Thanksgiving

RECIPES
Lou Seibert Pappas

PHOTOGRAPHS
Lara Hata

weldonowen

Contents

Thanksgiving Traditions

··

Many families begin the Thanksgiving meal by allowing each person at the table to list the reasons they are thankful. Every guest, young and old, takes a moment to give thanks. This and the many other traditions of Thanksgiving are what lend the holiday its cultural importance. More traditions are revealed in the recipes that make up the Thanksgiving table. Each dish, whether it's an uncle's favorite side dish or a neighbor's recipe for pumpkin pie, represents a specific memory, flavor, and regional touch that can often carry on for generations of Thanksgiving dinners to come. The task of preparing the meal can be daunting to any host, but the experience of serving a memorable feast to your loved ones is a rewarding one. Whether the challenge lies in feeding a large number of people or in having only one oven and many dishes to bake or roast, the key to preparing and hosting Thanksgiving dinner lies in being organized.

The first step is to determine the number and preferences of your guests. If you like, use the menu suggestions on pages 98–101 for inspiration. Once you've decided which dishes to prepare, think about the best serving style. Choose a casual family-style meal or a more formal tablesetting to suit your needs. Consider arranging the food on a buffet if you are expecting a large number of guests. Also, think about which beverages will work best with your menu. Once you know what you are serving and how, you can develop a timeline for each element to help plan your workload. Preparing a Thanksgiving feast can be a joy, and the meal an event. Use the suggestions and recipes in this book to create both a memorable holiday for others and a satisfying kitchen experience for yourself.

PLANNING THE FEAST
When planning the Thanksgiving meal, it is important to take into account the number and preferences of your guests. Once the guest list is finalized, you can create a work plan for yourself and a timeline for each task. Dividing tasks into items that can be done days or hours in advance will help you enjoy the holiday with your guests.

PREPARING THE KITCHEN
Once you have decided
on a menu, read through
all the recipes you will be
preparing a week or two
in advance. Use this time
to note which equipment
and ingredients you will
need to acquire. Plan your
shopping trips accordingly
to avoid the large crowds
and empty shelves sure
to come as Thanksgiving
Day approaches. It also
helps to know in advance
which serving vessels to
use and to be sure they
are warmed or chilled, as
needed, in advance.

PREPARING YOUR HOME
Have the linens cleaned
and pressed a week
before the holiday. Set
the table the night before
so that, on the day of the
feast, you can focus on
preparing the food and
enjoying the company
of your guests.

CASUAL VERSUS FORMAL STYLES

The terms casual and formal are too often misunderstood. Casual doesn't have to mean paper plates and napkins anymore than formal suggests a stiff demeanor and unwelcoming atmosphere. Rather, think of these serving styles in terms of making your meal easier to present, ensuring that your guests are comfortable, and generally offering the evening's repast at its best.

A casual meal will allow your guests to serve themselves portions of their own choosing and at intervals that work best for each individual. If there are a lot of children in attendance, a less strict mealtime and informal place-setting gives them a chance to entertain themselves while the adults dine at their own enjoyable pace. Family-style meals are one casual option which requires only easily passed serving dishes so each guest can partake of anything they wish.

Formal meals tend to be plated in the kitchen and brought to the table in courses, which allows you to showcase each part of the menu on its own and prolong the meal. While this does require a bit more last-minute work for the host, it can make a wonderful event for a smaller, more intimate group.

BUFFET-STYLE SERVING

Buffets are a great idea for crowds because they allow people to eat in shifts and plate their dishes to their preference. Guests can make their way through the buffet line, helping themselves to as much of each dish as they want. Once you set out the food, all you have to do is replenish the platters and dinnerware as needed. For large groups, set up a separate buffet station for self-serve beverages, such as wine and sparkling water or cider. Staging a buffet is one of the most popular serving styles for the holidays because it can be made either casual or formal and it can be tailored to suit both your home and your menu.

Every buffet should convey an abundance of food. Choose a table that is just large enough to hold everything you plan to serve and drape it with a tablecloth. Wrap the utensils in complementary napkins. Determine at which side of the table your guests will start, then place plates and bowls at the beginning and napkins and flatware at the end. Arrange the food in the order in which it should be eaten and provide serving utensils for each dish. Placing some items in footed bowls or on decorative pedestals will facilitate serving. For a finishing touch, place a seasonal centerpiece or flower arrangement on the table.

FESTIVE BEVERAGES

It isn't easy to find one wine that matches all the flavors of the Thanksgiving feast. One option is to serve both a white and a red wine. Try a crisp Chardonnay and a juicy Pinot Noir, which both pair well with most traditional holiday dishes. Or, use the ideas at right to find the perfect wines to match different parts of your menu. Plan on one bottle of wine for every two to three wine drinkers.

A tulip-shaped white wineglass and a larger, similarly shaped red wineglass are suitable for most wines. If you will be serving sparkling wine, use tall flutes, which trap bubbles and enhance effervescence. Choose lightweight, clear glasses that make a pinging sound when gently tapped.

It is wise to include a few nonalcoholic options, such as bottled sparkling or still water or iced tea, allowing one quart or liter for every two guests. Sparkling cider, hot spiced cider, and cranberry lemonade are festive beverages that everyone can enjoy.

PULLING IT ALL TOGETHER

Spending the time to plan all the details of your Thanksgiving dinner in advance will make the holiday itself a much smoother and more enjoyable one. A detailed checklist and timeline are both indispensable tools when you are hosting the event. Remember to shop well ahead of time, prepare as many dishes as you can early in the week, and have the table set before your guests arrive. For more tips on creating menus and work plans, turn to pages 98–101.

After Thanksgiving Day, you and your guests can indulge in leftovers for days to come. Package a variety of ingredients in tightly covered individual containers and send each guest home with both the makings and instructions for any of the recipes on pages 102–103.

Thanksgiving is a holiday for bringing together friends and family, young and old, to celebrate and be grateful for life's gifts. When the preparations are made, the cooking is completed, and the guests sit around the table, be sure to raise your glasses and give thanks for the delicious food and the warm company that surround you. No matter if this is the first Thanksgiving you've hosted or if you have many years of experience, the recipes and suggestions throughout this book will help ensure that the occasion goes smoothly. Perhaps, too, you will discover new flavors and ingredients for your Thanksgiving table.

WINE PAIRING MADE EASY

Appetizers
Sparkling whites and Champagne are classic aperitifs that enhance a variety of savory flavors.

Turkey and other poultry
Crisp Chardonnay is a crowd-pleaser that pairs well with white meat. A medium-bodied Pinot Noir, low in tannins and slightly chilled, will contribute a fruity flavor.

Ham and smoked meats
Medium-bodied whites and reds like Riesling, Pinot Gris, or Pinot Noir complement ham's smoky richness.

Soups
Pairing wine with soups can be tricky. Try a dry sherry, such as a fino or manzanilla.

Salads
A Sauvignon Blanc or similar high-acid white wine will counter the acid in salad dressings.

11

Starters

Crostini with Tapenade	15
Stuffed Roasted Figs	16
Roasted Onion Soup	17
Curried Butternut Squash Soup	18
Persimmon & Arugula Salad	20
Fennel & Orange Salad	21
Watercress, Endive & Apple Salad	22
Beet & Green Bean Salad	25

Crostini with Tapenade

The crostini can be stored in an airtight container at room temperature for 3 days. The tapenade will keep in the refrigerator for 10 days. Use any leftover olive spread as a flavorful filling for celery sticks.

Preheat the oven to 325°F. Spread the pine nuts on a small, shallow pan and toast, stirring once or twice to prevent scorching, until fragrant and slightly darkened, 8–10 minutes. Pour onto a plate to cool.

Leave the oven on and at 325°F. Arrange the bread slices on 2 rimmed baking sheets and brush the tops lightly with oil. Toast in the oven until golden brown, 8–10 minutes. Let cool.

In a food processor, combine the toasted pine nuts, olives, green onions, parsley, garlic, lemon zest, lemon juice, vinegar, mustard, and cheese and process until minced. Add the 2 tablespoons oil and process until combined. Transfer the tapenade to a bowl, season to taste with pepper, cover tightly, and refrigerate for at least 2 hours to allow the flavors to blend. You should have about 1¼ cups.

Spread the crostini with a thin layer of the tapenade, dividing it evenly, and arrange on one or more platters. Serve right away.

Pine nuts, ½ cup

Slender baguettes, 2, thinly sliced on the diagonal

Olive oil for brushing, plus 2 tablespoons

Pitted green olives, 1¼ cups (about 6 ounces)

Green onions, 2, including tender green tops, chopped

Fresh flat-leaf parsley, ¼ cup minced

Garlic, 2 cloves, chopped

Lemon zest, 3 or 4 narrow strips, each 3–4 inches long, coarsely chopped

Fresh lemon juice, 1 tablespoon

Balsamic vinegar, 1 tablespoon

Dijon mustard, 1 tablespoon

Pecorino Romano cheese, ¼ cup freshly grated

Freshly ground pepper

Stuffed Roasted Figs

You can assemble these delectable mouthfuls in the morning and refrigerate them for up to 4 hours. Let the figs stand at room temperature for about 30 minutes before roasting and serving them.

MAKES 16 APPETIZERS; 8 SERVINGS

Black Mission figs, 8, halved lengthwise and pits removed

Soft fresh goat cheese, 3 ounces

Fresh rosemary, 1 tablespoon finely chopped

Pancetta, 2 ounces, thinly sliced, cut into sixteen 1½-inch pieces

Preheat the oven to 375°F. Line 2 rimmed baking sheets with parchment paper.

Spoon about 1½ teaspoons of the cheese onto the cut side of each fig half, pressing it gently in place. Sprinkle the cheese evenly with the rosemary, and wrap each fig half with a piece of pancetta. Arrange the halves, cut sides up, on the prepared baking sheet.

Roast the figs until the pancetta is lightly browned and the figs are heated through, 6–8 minutes. Divide the stuffed figs evenly among small plates and serve right away.

Roasted Onion Soup

Roasting the onions before blending them with the broth gives French onion soup a caramelized flavor. You can prepare this soup, prior to adding the bread and cheese, up to 1 day in advance.

MAKES 6 SERVINGS

Preheat the oven to 375°F. Line 2 rimmed baking sheets with parchment paper.

In a large bowl, toss the onions with the oil and vinegar, then scatter the onions evenly in the prepared pan. Roast, turning several times, until golden brown on the edges, 30–35 minutes. Remove from the oven.

Preheat the broiler. In a large pot over medium-high heat, bring the broth to a rapid simmer. Add the onions, reduce the heat, and simmer for 15 minutes to blend the flavors. Add salt and pepper to taste. (If making this soup in advance, cool it and refrigerate, tightly covered, for up to 1 day. Reheat over low heat before proceeding.)

Arrange six 8-ounce flameproof soup bowls on a rimmed baking sheet. Ladle the soup into the bowls, dividing evenly, and float a bread slice on each serving. Mix together the cheeses and sprinkle on the bread slices.

Place the baking sheet under the broiler and broil until the cheese melts and lightly browns, about 2 minutes. Serve right away.

Large yellow onions, 5, thinly sliced

Olive oil, 2 tablespoons

Balsamic vinegar, 1 tablespoon

Reduced-sodium beef broth, 6 cups

Salt and freshly ground pepper

Country-style bread, 6 slices, each ½ inch thick, toasted

Parmesan cheese, ½ cup freshly grated

Gruyère cheese, ½ cup finely shredded

Curried Butternut Squash Soup

The subtle sweetness of apple and the exotic flavor of curry powder elevate this creamy soup.
Roasting the fruit and vegetables gives them a caramelized taste and enriches the final result.

MAKES 8–10 SERVINGS

Canola oil, 3 tablespoons

Balsamic vinegar,
2 tablespoons

Butternut squash,
2, about 3 pounds total
weight, halved lengthwise
and seeded

Large Granny Smith apple,
1, peeled, halved, and cored

Yellow onions, 2, quartered

**Reduced-sodium chicken
broth,** 6 cups

Curry powder, 1 tablespoon

Ground cumin, 1 teaspoon

Cayenne pepper to taste
(optional)

Half-and-half or plain
yogurt, ½ cup

**Salt and freshly ground
black pepper**

Walnut pieces for garnish
(optional)

Red pepper flakes for
garnish (optional)

Preheat the oven to 375°F. Line 2 rimmed baking sheets with aluminum foil.

In a small bowl, stir together the oil and vinegar. Brush the cut sides of the squash, the apple halves, and the onions with the oil mixture. Place the squash and apple halves, cut sides down, and the onions on the prepared baking sheet. Bake, turning the fruit and vegetables once or twice, until tender and lightly browned, about 30 minutes for the apple and 45–50 minutes for the vegetables. Transfer to a cutting board and let cool. Scoop out the flesh from the squash halves, discarding the peel. Coarsely chop the apple and onions.

Transfer the squash flesh and onion and apple pieces to a large saucepan and add the broth, curry powder, cumin, and cayenne pepper, if using. Bring to a boil over medium-high heat and then reduce the heat to medium. Simmer until very tender, about 20 minutes. Remove from the heat and let cool. In a blender, purée the soup in batches until smooth. Return the soup to the pan, stir in the half-and-half, season to taste with salt and black pepper, and heat through over medium heat. (The soup can be prepared up to 2 days in advance and stored, tightly covered, in the refrigerator. Heat through before serving.)

Ladle the soup into warmed bowls and garnish with the walnut pieces and red pepper flakes, if using.

Persimmon & Arugula Salad

The addition of bright orange persimmons lends an autumnal touch to this salad of peppery arugula and creamy goat cheese. Buy Fuyu persimmons, which are firmer and smaller than the soft Hachiya.

MAKES 6 SERVINGS

Slivered blanched almonds, ½ cup

Balsamic vinegar, 2 tablespoons

Dijon mustard, 1 teaspoon

Extra-virgin olive oil, 3 tablespoons

Salt and freshly ground pepper

Arugula leaves, 8 cups

Fuyu persimmons, 2, cored

Soft fresh goat cheese, 3 ounces, cut into 6 slices

Preheat the oven to 350°F. Spread the almonds on a small, shallow pan and toast, stirring once or twice to prevent scorching, until fragrant and slightly darkened, 8–10 minutes. Pour onto a plate to cool.

In a small bowl, whisk together the vinegar and mustard until blended. Whisk in the oil and salt and pepper to taste. In a large bowl, toss the arugula with the dressing until evenly coated.

Divide the dressed arugula among salad plates. Thinly slice the persimmons crosswise through the stem end and fan the slices on top of the greens. Top each with a slice of cheese and a scattering of toasted almonds and serve right away.

Fennel & Orange Salad

Fennel adds a subtle licorice flavor to this zesty orange salad. Use a mandoline to shave the fennel, or cut it into slivers with a sharp knife. Seeded mandarin oranges can be used in place of the navels.

MAKES 6 SERVINGS

To make the dressing, in a small bowl, whisk together the vinegar, lemon juice, and mustard until blended. Whisk in the oil, shallot, and salt and pepper to taste.

Working with 1 orange at a time, cut a slice off the top and bottom to reveal the flesh. Stand the fruit upright. Using a sharp knife, thickly slice away the peel and pith, cutting downward and following the natural contour of the fruit. Holding the fruit over a bowl, cut along either side of each section of flesh, freeing it from its membrane and dropping the flesh into the bowl. Repeat this process with the remaining oranges.

In a large salad bowl, toss together the greens and shaved fennel. Drizzle on the dressing and mix lightly. Scatter the oranges on top and sprinkle with the cheese. Serve right away.

DRESSING

Champagne vinegar, 2 tablespoons

Fresh lemon juice, 1 tablespoon

Dijon mustard, 2 teaspoons

Extra-virgin olive oil, ¼ cup

Shallot, 1, minced

Salt and freshly ground pepper

Navel oranges, 3

Mixed salad greens such as arugula leaves, frisée, mâche, and watercress, 8 cups

Fennel bulb, 1, trimmed, halved lengthwise, and finely shaved or slivered

Aged sheep's milk cheese such as *Manchego* or *Petit Basque*, 2 ounces, crumbled

Watercress, Endive & Apple Salad

Peppery watercress and bitter endive are nicely offset with tart-sweet green apples. The rich, robust flavor of hazelnuts provides a nice accent in both the salad dressing and sprinkled on top.

Hazelnuts, ⅔ cup

Watercress, 3 large bunches, about 1½ pounds total weight, tough stems removed

Belgian endive, 3 heads, about 1 pound total weight, cored and separated into leaves

Hazelnut oil or extra-virgin olive oil, 5 tablespoons

Salt and freshly ground pepper

White balsamic vinegar, 3 tablespoons

Granny Smith apples, 2

Preheat the oven to 375°F. Spread the hazelnuts in a shallow metal pan, place in the oven, and toast, stirring once or twice, until crisp, fragrant, and brown, about 10 minutes. Wrap the hot nuts in a clean kitchen towel and let steam for 1 minute, then vigorously roll the wrapped nuts between the palms of your hands until most of the dark brown skins are removed. Pick the nuts out of the debris of the peels and coarsely chop them. (The nuts can be toasted and skinned 1 day ahead; store in an airtight container at room temperature. Chop them just before completing the salad.)

In a large serving bowl, toss together the watercress and endive. Drizzle with the oil and toss. Sprinkle about ½ teaspoon salt over the greens and toss again. Add the hazelnuts, vinegar, and about ½ teaspoon pepper and mix well. Taste and adjust the seasonings.

Halve and core the apples and cut each half lengthwise into eighths. Add to the bowl with the greens and toss to mix. Serve right away.

Beet & Green Bean Salad

Here is a wonderful mix of colors, textures, and flavors to launch any holiday meal. If you like, you can cook the beans and beets up to 1 day in advance and toast the nuts 3–4 days before the meal.

MAKES 6 SERVINGS

Preheat the oven to 350°F. Spread the walnuts on a small, shallow pan and toast, stirring once or twice to prevent scorching, until fragrant and slightly darkened, 8–10 minutes. Pour onto a plate to cool.

Trim the beets, leaving 1 inch of the stem intact, but do not peel. Pour water to a depth of 1 inch into a saucepan, season with salt, bring to a boil over high heat, and add the beets. Cover, reduce the heat to low, and simmer until the beets are tender, 20–25 minutes. Drain and let cool completely. Peel the beets, slice thickly, and place in a large bowl.

Meanwhile, bring a saucepan three-fourths full of water to a boil over high heat, season with salt, add the beans, and cook until tender-crisp, 4–5 minutes. Drain and immediately immerse in cold water to halt the cooking. Drain again, pat dry, and add to the bowl with the beets.

In a small bowl, whisk together the vinegar and mustard until blended. Whisk in the oil and salt and pepper to taste. Pour over the beets and beans and toss to coat. Add the arugula and toss again lightly.

Arrange the salad on a chilled serving platter. Scatter the walnuts and cheese over the top and serve right away.

Walnut halves, ½ cup

Large yellow beets, 4, each about 3 inches in diameter

Salt and freshly ground pepper

Young, slender green beans or haricots verts, ¾ pound, ends trimmed

Balsamic vinegar, 2 tablespoons

Dijon mustard, 1 teaspoon

Extra-virgin olive oil, 3 tablespoons

Arugula leaves or young, tender salad greens, 2 cups

Ricotta salata **cheese,** 2 ounces, crumbled

Main Dishes

Classic Roast Turkey

This recipe uses a compound butter flavored with fresh herbs and orange zest. Spreading the butter both under and over the bird's skin helps keep the meat moist and flavorful and the skin crisp.

MAKES 12–15 SERVINGS

About 2 hours before roasting, remove the turkey from the refrigerator. Remove the giblets and neck from the turkey cavity. Reserve the liver for another use or discard. If you like, refrigerate the neck, gizzard, and heart to make stock or Giblet Gravy (page 50) or discard. Pull out the pale yellow pads of fat in the body cavity on both sides of the tail and discard.

Position a rack in the lower third of the oven and preheat to 325°F.

Pat the turkey dry with paper towels. Fold the wings underneath the back of the turkey to prevent their over-browning in the oven. Season the cavity and skin of the turkey lightly with salt and pepper. Stuff the turkey (see page 42) and truss it (see page 105) if desired.

To make the herbed orange butter, combine the butter, orange zest, sage, rosemary, and a pinch each of salt and pepper in a bowl. Mash the ingredients together with a fork or spoon. (The herbed orange butter can be prepared up to 3 days in advance, covered tightly, and refrigerated. It can also be frozen for up to 1 month. Allow it to sit at room temperature to soften before using.)

Working from the tail end of the turkey, gently slide your fingers between the skin and flesh on the breast, legs, and as much of the thighs as you can. Next, from the neck end, slide your fingers between the skin and breast of the turkey. Once the skin is loosened, using your fingers, carefully spread about half of the herbed orange butter under the skin and over the meat on the turkey breast, legs, and thighs, distributing it as evenly as possible. Spread the remaining butter all over the outside of the skin, again distributing it as evenly as possible.

continued...

Fresh whole turkey,
1, about 12 pounds

Salt and freshly ground pepper

HERBED ORANGE BUTTER

Unsalted butter, 1/2 cup, at room temperature

Orange zest, 2 tablespoons minced

Fresh sage,
2 teaspoons minced

Fresh rosemary,
2 teaspoons minced

Canola oil for brushing

Yellow onion, 1, quartered

Orange, 1, quartered

Carrots, 3, coarsely chopped

Pan Gravy (page 31) or other gravy (optional)

Whole fresh fruit such as apricots and kumquats for garnish (optional)

Whole sage leaves for garnish (optional)

FLAVORING THE TURKEY
The compound butter used here is one classic technique for flavoring poultry. Combining room temperature butter with herbs and other seasonings creates the perfect mixure to rub under and over the skin before cooking. As the turkey roasts, the butter melts into the flesh, keeping the meat moist and creating a crisp, golden-brown skin. Another way to add flavor is with a flavor injector, a kitchen tool used to insert marinade deep into the meat of the bird. Injectors are stainless-steel, easy-to-handle syringes filled with liquid marinade. When the needle pierces the turkey skin, the liquid is plunged throughout the flesh, keeping the turkey moist during cooking and imparting complex layers of flavor.

Select a flameproof roasting pan just large enough to hold the turkey. (For more information on choosing the pan, see page 34.) Lightly brush the roasting rack with canola oil and place the turkey on the rack. Place the pan in the oven and roast the turkey, rotating the pan's position on the oven rack from front to back several times for more even cooking, for $1^3/4$ hours.

Add the onion, orange, and carrots to the pan and continue to roast, stirring the orange and the vegetables occasionally, until a thermometer inserted into the thickest part of the turkey thigh away from the bone registers 175°F and into the thickest part of the turkey breast away from the bone, several inches above the wings, registers 165°F (see page 106), about $1^1/4$ hours longer, for a total roasting time of about 3 hours.

Remove the turkey from the oven. Insert a sturdy, large, metal spoon into the body cavity, and, supporting the turkey at the neck cavity with a carving fork, tilt it so that the juices in the cavity flow into the roasting pan. Transfer the turkey, breast side up, to a carving board (a cutting board with a groove to capture poultry juices). Let the bird rest for at least 20 minutes and up to 45 minutes, tenting with aluminum foil if needed to keep it warm. This resting period, which allows the juices to redistribute evenly throughout the flesh, is a key element in achieving a juicy turkey.

If you like, place the roasting pan with the pan juices and vegetables over 2 burners to prepare the Pan Gravy (page 31), Giblet Gravy (page 50), or Herbed Citrus Gravy (page 51).

Have ready a heated platter to hold the carved turkey. If you have used string to truss the bird, snip it with kitchen scissors and discard it. Carve the turkey (see page 107) and arrange it on the platter. Garnish with the fruits and herbs, if desired. Serve the turkey, asking your guests whether they prefer dark meat (from the leg and thigh), white meat (from the breast), or a combination.

Pan Gravy

Although it takes less time to make this fast turkey stock than if you were making it from scratch, you can use 7 cups of high-quality, reduced-sodium chicken stock from a specialty-food store in its place.

MAKES 12–15 SERVINGS

To make the turkey stock, warm the oil in a stockpot over medium-high heat. Add the drumettes and brown well, turning once or twice, about 15 minutes. Stir in the vegetables and herbs. Reduce the heat to low, cover, and cook, scraping the browned bits from the bottom of the pot occasionally, about 15 minutes. Add the broth, sherry, and salt and pepper to taste and bring to a simmer. Cover partially and cook for 35 minutes. Strain the stock through a sieve into a large bowl. If using right away, spoon off the visible fat or pour through a fat separator. Otherwise, cool for 30 minutes, then cover and refrigerate for up to overnight. Using a large spoon, remove the solid fat from the top and discard. (You will have about 7 cups of finished stock; it can be refrigerated for up to 3 days or frozen for up to 3 months.)

To make the gravy, pour the pan drippings into a fat separator and let stand for a few minutes until the fat rises to the top. Pour the pan juices into a large glass measuring cup; reserve the fat in the separator. Add turkey stock to the measuring cup to reach 7 cups. Reserve the extra stock for another use.

Place the roasting pan on 2 burners over medium heat. Measure out $2/3$ cup of the reserved fat and add it to the pan, adding melted butter to make up the difference. Sprinkle in the flour, whisk well, and cook, whisking, until the raw flour smell is gone, about 2 minutes. Increase the heat to medium-high. Pour in the stock mixture and bring to a boil, scraping up the browned bits on the bottom. Reduce the heat to medium low and simmer, whisking often, until it has thickened, about 10 minutes. Season with salt and pepper, pour into a warmed sauceboat or bowl with a ladle, and serve with the turkey.

QUICK TURKEY STOCK

Peanut oil or canola oil, 3 tablespoons

Turkey wing drumettes, 2

Yellow onion, 3 cups chopped

Carrots, 2 cups chopped

Celery, 1 cup chopped

Fresh parsley, 1 bunch

Fresh thyme sprigs, 2

Bay leaves, 2

Reduced-sodium chicken broth, 8 cups

Dry sherry, $3/4$ cup

Salt and freshly ground pepper

Melted unsalted butter (optional)

All-purpose flour, $2/3$ cup

Apple-Brined Turkey Breasts

Brining turkey, or soaking it in this salt-and-sugar solution, adds moisture to the meat. It is an especially good technique to use with all-white breast meat, which can become dry with roasting.

MAKES 12–15 SERVINGS

Make the Apple Brine as directed on page 35.

Pat the turkey breasts dry with paper towels. Immerse the turkey breasts completely in the stockpot with the brine. If needed, invert a small plate on top of the turkey breasts to keep them submerged. Alternatively, if using a brining bag, put the turkey breasts in the bag, slowly pour the brine in over them, close the bag (squeezing out the excess air), and place in a large bowl. Cover and refrigerate the turkey breasts in the brine for 12–24 hours, turning them occasionally in the brine. Drain and discard the brine. Cover the turkey breasts with fresh, cold water and let stand at room temperature, turning once or twice, for an additional 4 hours. Drain the water and pat the turkey breasts dry. Trim any excess skin from the turkey breasts.

Position a rack in the lower third of the oven and preheat to 325°F.

Use your fingertips to spread 1½ tablespoons of the butter over the skin of each turkey breast, distributing it as evenly as possible. Quarter the onion and coarsely chop the carrots. Select a flameproof roasting pan just large enough to hold the turkey breasts. (For more information on choosing the pan, see page 34.) Lightly brush the roasting rack with canola oil and place the turkey breasts on the rack. Scatter the onion and carrot pieces in the pan around the turkey. Roast, rotating the pan's position on the oven rack from front to back once for more even cooking, for 30 minutes.

Meanwhile, in a small saucepan, combine the chicken broth, the remaining 6 tablespoons butter, the white wine, ¼ cup canola oil, and the lemon juice.

continued...

Apple Brine (page 35)

Fresh whole bone-in turkey breasts, 2, about 12 pounds total weight

Unsalted butter, 9 tablespoons, at room temperature

Yellow onion, 1, unpeeled

Large carrots, 2, unpeeled

Canola oil, ¼ cup, plus more for brushing

Reduced-sodium chicken broth, 1¾ cups

Dry white wine, ½ cup

Fresh lemon juice, 1 tablespoon

CHOOSING THE PAN
Using a heavy roasting
pan will help keep the
juices from burning.
Avoid nonstick pans,
which won't develop as
many browned bits to
help flavor the gravy. If
you are using a disposable
foil pan, buy 2 and double
up for extra strength.
A metal rack will keep
the turkey bottom from
stewing in the drippings
and sticking to the pan.
You can use a wire cake
rack in a pinch, but a V-
shaped nonstick roasting
rack is best because it
will also ease the removal
of the turkey from the pan;
be sure to oil the rack well.
For a 10- to 14-pound
turkey, a 14-by-10-by-
2½-inch pan is best; for
16–20 pounds, choose a
17-by-11½-by-2½-inch
pan; for 24 pounds and
over, use a 19-by-14-by-
3¼-inch pan.

Warm the broth mixture over low heat until the butter has melted. When the turkey breasts have roasted for about 30 minutes, baste them with some of the broth mixture.

Continue to roast the turkey breasts, basting about every 30 minutes with the remaining broth mixture and then with the accumulated pan juices, rotating the pan's position and stirring the vegetables in the pan occasionally, until the breasts are well browned and a thermometer inserted into the thickest part of the breast away from the bone registers 165°F (see page 106), about 2 hours total roasting time. (Turkey breast is very lean, so it dries out and toughens easily when cooked beyond 170°F.)

Using tongs, transfer the turkey breasts, skin side up, to a carving board (a cutting board with a groove to capture poultry juices). Let the breasts rest for 10 minutes, tenting with aluminum foil if needed to keep them warm. This resting period, which allows the juices to redistribute evenly throughout the flesh, is a key element in achieving a juicy turkey breast.

If you like, place the roasting pan with the pan juices and vegetables over 2 burners to prepare the Herbed Citrus Gravy (page 51), Giblet Gravy (page 50), or Pan Gravy (page 31).

Have ready a warmed serving platter. Hold a carving fork in one hand to brace one of the turkey breasts. Using a thin, flexible carving knife, cut the breast meat away from the rib cage in a single piece. Working across the length of the breast, cut the meat against the grain into slices about ½ inch thick. As the slices are cut, arrange them on the warmed platter. Repeat to carve the second turkey breast and serve right away.

Apple Brine

The mixture of apple juice, salt, honey, and sugar used here puts a fruity, flavorful spin on the usual brine combinations. It also complements the sweet condiments on the Thanksgiving table.

MAKES BRINE FOR TWO 5- TO 6-POUND TURKEY BREASTS

Apple juice or sweet apple cider, 3 quarts, chilled

Kosher salt, 2 cups

Honey, ½ cup

Granulated sugar, ½ cup

Brown sugar, ½ cup firmly packed

If using a stockpot: Combine the apple juice, 3 quarts water, the salt, honey, granulated sugar, and brown sugar in a nonreactive stockpot about 3 inches taller and wider than the turkey breasts. (A large stockpot made of stainless steel or anodized metal—not uncoated aluminum—is a good choice.) Place over medium-high heat and bring to a boil, stirring to dissolve the salt. Remove from the heat and let cool completely. Use as directed on page 33.

If using a brining bag: Combine the apple juice, 3 quarts water, the salt, honey, granulated sugar, and brown sugar in a nonreactive 7-quart saucepan made of stainless steel or anodized metal. Place over medium-high heat and bring to a boil, stirring to dissolve the salt. Remove from the heat and let cool completely. Use as directed on page 33.

For more details on brining, see page 104.

Hickory-Smoked Turkey

Expect the meat of this turkey to have a pinkish color, as is typical for home-smoked birds. Cooked mainly on the grill, this turkey leaves the oven free for pies, gratins, and other baked dishes.

MAKES 12–15 SERVINGS

The day before you plan to prepare the turkey, place the hickory wood pieces in a bowl and add enough water to cover them completely. The hickory wood must be soaked for 24 hours so it will smolder, and not ignite, in the grill, creating a lot of smoke to infuse the turkey. Do not drain the hickory wood until just before grilling.

About 2 hours before grilling, remove the turkey from the refrigerator. Remove the giblets and neck from the turkey cavity. Reserve the liver for another use or discard. If you like, refrigerate the neck, gizzard, and heart to make stock or Giblet Gravy (page 50) or discard. Pull out the pale yellow pads of fat in the body cavity on both sides of the tail and discard.

Pat the turkey dry with paper towels. Fold the wings underneath the back of the turkey to prevent their over-browning in the oven. Season the cavity and skin of the turkey lightly with salt and pepper. Truss the turkey (see page 105), if desired, for a compact shape.

Light a fire in a large charcoal grill with a cover. When the coals are white, bank them on two sides of the fire bed to create a cool zone in the center. Drain the hickory wood and place 3 chunks atop each bank of coals. Put the grill rack in place and cover the grill. Heat the grill until a built-in grill thermometer or oven thermometer placed inside the grill registers 250°F.

Put the turkey in a flameproof roasting pan and place on the grill rack over the cool zone. Cover the grill and cook the turkey, rotating the pan occasionally to expose the bird evenly to the smoke, for 3 hours. During this time, uncover

continued...

Hickory wood, six 3-inch chunks

Fresh whole turkey, 1, about 12 pounds

Salt and freshly ground pepper

Lady apples for garnish (optional)

Whole nuts for garnish (optional)

Horseradish-Apple Sauce (page 39; optional)

SELECTING A TURKEY
Fresh turkeys are easy to
find during the holidays
and taste much better
than frozen turkeys. If
possible, choose a free-
range, organic turkey.
When calculating what
size turkey you'll need,
figure on ¾-pound per
person, and twice that
for leftovers. Pick up a
fresh turkey the day
before it is to be prepared,
and store it in the coldest
part of the refrigerator.
Thaw frozen turkeys in the
refrigerator to prevent
bacteria from multiplying.
Plan on 3–4 hours per
pound for turkey to thaw.
(It may take 2–3 days for
a frozen turkey to thaw.)
Roast thawed turkey
within 2 days and do
not refreeze it.

the grill no more than is necessary (to avoid heat loss) and maintain its temperature at about 250°F, regulating the level by adjusting the upper and lower vents. Light more charcoal briquettes in a chimney starter and add them to the grill as needed to maintain the heat.

Near the end of the 3-hour period, preheat the oven to 325°F. Transfer the turkey from the grill to the oven without allowing it to cool. Roast the turkey, rotating the pan's position on the oven rack from front to back several times for more even cooking, until a thermometer inserted into the thickest part of the turkey thigh away from the bone registers 175°F and into the thickest part of the turkey breast away from the bone, several inches above the wings, registers 165°F (see page 106), 30–40 minutes. Do not overcook.

Remove the turkey from the oven. Insert a sturdy, large, metal spoon into the body cavity, and, supporting the turkey at the neck cavity with a carving fork, tilt it so that the juices in the cavity flow into the roasting pan. Transfer the turkey, breast side up, to a carving board (a cutting board with a groove to capture poultry juices). Let the bird rest for at least 20 minutes and up to 45 minutes, tenting with aluminum foil if needed to keep it warm. This resting period, which allows the juices to redistribute evenly throughout the flesh, is a key element in achieving a juicy turkey.

Have ready a heated platter to hold the carved turkey. If you have used string to truss the bird, snip it with kitchen scissors and discard it. Carve the turkey (see page 107) and arrange it on the platter, garnishing with the lady apples and whole nuts if desired. Serve the turkey with the Horseradish-Apple Sauce (opposite) alongside, asking your guests whether they prefer dark meat (from the leg and thigh), white meat (from the breast), or a combination.

Horseradish-Apple Sauce

The pan juices from a smoked turkey are too potent to turn into a gravy. Instead, make this spicy and creamy sauce to serve alongside. You do not need to peel the apple before grating it.

MAKES 12–15 SERVINGS

Grate the apple flesh coarsely with a handheld grater, avoiding the core. Finely snip the fresh chives until you have about 1 tablespoon.

In a bowl, stir together the horseradish, sour cream, and mayonnaise. Add the grated apple, the snipped chives, and the sugar to the horseradish mixture and stir until combined. Season with pepper to taste.

Cover and refrigerate the sauce until ready to serve. (The sauce can be stored, tightly covered in the refrigerator, for up to 3 days.) Serve cold.

Red apple, 1

Fresh chives, 1 bunch

Prepared cream-style horseradish, 16 ounces

Sour cream, ½ cup

Mayonnaise, ½ cup

Sugar, 1 teaspoon

Freshly ground pepper

Herb-Brined Turkey

Brining creates moist, juicy flesh while enhancing flavor. Two points are crucial: choose a container just large enough to hold the turkey during brining and be sure to dissolve the sugar and salt completely.

MAKES 12–15 SERVINGS

Make the Herb Brine as directed on page 43.

About 2 hours before brining, remove the turkey from the refrigerator. Remove the giblets and neck from the turkey cavity. Reserve the liver for another use or discard. If you like, refrigerate the neck, gizzard, and heart to make stock or Giblet Gravy (page 50) or discard. Pull out the pale yellow pads of fat in the body cavity on both sides of the tail and discard.

Pat the turkey dry with paper towels. Immerse the turkey completely, breast side down, in the stockpot with the brine. If needed, invert a small plate on top of the turkey to keep it submerged. Alternatively, if using a brining bag, put the turkey in the bag, slowly pour the brine in over it, close the bag (squeezing out the excess air), and place in a large bowl. Cover and refrigerate the turkey in the brine for 12–24 hours.

Remove the turkey from the brine, rinse inside and out, and pat dry with paper towels. Let the turkey stand at room temperature for about 1 hour before roasting. Fold the wings underneath the back of the turkey to prevent their over-browning in the oven. Season the cavity and skin of the turkey with salt and pepper. Stuff the turkey (see page 42) and truss it (see page 105) if desired.

Position a rack in the lower third of the oven and preheat to 325°F.

Select a flameproof roasting pan just large enough to hold the turkey. (For more information on choosing the pan, see page 34.) Lightly brush the roasting rack with canola oil and place the turkey on the rack. Place the pan in the

continued...

Herb Brine (page 43)

Fresh whole turkey, 1, about 12 pounds

Salt and freshly ground pepper

Canola oil for brushing

Yellow onion, 1, quartered

Carrots, 3, coarsely chopped

Celery stalk, 1, with some leaves, coarsely chopped

Pan Gravy (page 31) or other gravy (optional)

Lemons for garnish (optional)

Fresh marjoram sprigs for garnish (optional)

oven and roast the turkey, rotating the pan's position on the oven rack from front to back several times for more even cooking, for 1³/₄ hours.

Add the onion, carrots, and celery to the pan and continue to roast, stirring the vegetables occasionally, until a thermometer inserted into the thickest part of the turkey thigh away from the bone registers 175°F and into the thickest part of the turkey breast away from the bone, several inches above the wings, registers 165°F (see page 106), about 1¹/₄ hours longer, for a total roasting time of about 3 hours.

Remove the turkey from the oven. Insert a sturdy, large, metal spoon into the body cavity, and, supporting the turkey at the neck cavity with a carving fork, tilt it so that the juices in the cavity flow into the roasting pan. Transfer the turkey, breast side up, to a carving board (a cutting board with a groove to capture poultry juices). Let the bird rest for at least 20 minutes and up to 45 minutes, tenting with aluminum foil if needed to keep it warm. This resting period, which allows the juices to redistribute evenly throughout the flesh, is a key element in achieving a juicy turkey.

If you like, place the roasting pan with the pan juices and vegetables over 2 burners to prepare the Pan Gravy (page 31), Giblet Gravy (page 50), or Herbed Citrus Gravy (page 51).

Have ready a heated platter to hold the carved turkey. If you have used string to truss the bird, snip it with kitchen scissors and discard it. Carve the turkey (see page 107) and arrange it on the platter, garnishing with the lemon slices and marjoram if desired. Serve the turkey, asking your guests whether they prefer dark meat (from the leg and thigh), white meat (from the breast), or a combination.

Herb Brine

This flavorful brine pairs the woodsy flavor of rosemary with the clean flavor of parsley, but you can substitute or add any number of fresh herbs for those used in this recipe.

MAKES BRINE FOR ONE 10- TO 12-POUND TURKEY

If using a stockpot: Combine the salt, sugar, and 6 quarts of room-temperature water in a nonreactive stockpot about 3 inches taller and wider than the turkey. (A large stockpot made of stainless steel or anodized metal—not uncoated aluminum—is a good choice.) Stir until the salt and sugar dissolve; this will take several minutes. Add the lemon, rosemary, coriander, parsley sprigs, peppercorns, and bay leaves and stir well. Use as directed on page 41.

If using a brining bag: Combine the salt, sugar, and 6 quarts of room-temperature water in a nonreactive 7-quart saucepan made of stainless steel or anodized metal. Stir until the salt and sugar dissolve; this could take several minutes. Add the lemon slices, rosemary, coriander, parsley sprigs, peppercorns, and bay leaves and stir well. Use as directed on page 41.

For more details on brining, see page 104.

Kosher salt, 1 cup

Sugar, 1 cup

Lemon, 1, thinly sliced

Fresh rosemary sprig, 1

Coriander seeds, ½ teaspoon

Flat-leaf parsley sprigs, 8

Peppercorns, 10

Bay leaves, 2

Cider-Glazed Baked Ham

A baked ham is a festive alternative to the traditional Thanksgiving turkey. Use a cooked, smoked ham, often labeled "water added," not a country or dry-aged ham. You may need to order it in advance.

MAKES 10–12 SERVINGS

Fully cooked bone-in smoked ham, 1, about 18 pounds

Brandy, 1 cup

Unfiltered apple cider, 1 cup

Honey, ¾ cup

Position a rack in the lower third of the oven and preheat to 325°F. Slice away the rind (if any) and most of the fat from the upper surface of the ham, leaving a layer of fat about ¼ inch thick. With a sharp knife, shallowly score the upper surface of the ham with diagonal cuts about 2 inches apart.

Place the ham on a rack in a shallow roasting pan just large enough to hold it comfortably. Add about 3 cups of water to the roasting pan and place it in the oven. Bake for 2¼ hours.

Meanwhile, in a glass measuring cup, stir together the brandy, cider, and honey. After 2¼ hours of baking, pour off the water from the roasting pan. Baste the ham with about one-third of the brandy mixture and bake for 12 minutes. Continue to bake, basting the ham with the brandy mixture (first from the measuring cup and then from the bottom of the roasting pan), at 12-minute intervals until the ham is glazed and shiny, for another 45 minutes or so (for a total baking time of about 3 hours).

Let the ham rest on a cutting board for 15 minutes. (Since the ham is as good warm as it is hot, and since it stays hot for at least 1 hour after baking, don't hesitate to let it rest, uncarved, while you use the oven for side dishes.) Carve the ham into thin slices and serve hot or warm.

Herb-Roasted Chicken

If your gathering is small, a roasted chicken—even two—can be a nice alternative to a large turkey. Here, the bird is simply flavored with butter and fresh rosemary to let its natural flavor shine through.

MAKES 4 SERVINGS

Whole chicken, 1, about 4 pounds

Unsalted butter, 2 tablespoons at room temperature and 2 tablespoons chilled

Salt and freshly ground pepper

Fresh rosemary, 2 sprigs

Canola oil for brushing

About 30 minutes before roasting, remove the chicken from the refrigerator. Pull out and discard the yellow pads of fat from both sides of the body cavity.

Position a rack in the center of the oven and preheat it to 450°F.

Pat the chicken dry with paper towels. Using your fingers, rub the outside of the chicken with the 2 tablespoons room-temperature butter, distributing it as evenly as possible. Sprinkle salt and pepper evenly over the inside and outside of the chicken. Slip the rosemary sprigs into the cavity and then truss the chicken (see page 105), if desired.

Select a flameproof roasting pan just large enough to hold the chicken. Lightly brush the roasting rack with canola oil and place the chicken on the rack. Place the chicken on its back on the oiled rack in the pan and roast for 15 minutes. Remove from the oven, insert a sturdy, large, metal spoon into the cavity and use it turn the chicken onto one of its sides. Return the chicken to the oven. Reduce the oven temperature to 375°F and roast for 30 minutes. Turn the chicken onto its other side and continue roasting until a thermometer inserted into the thickest part of the chicken thigh away from the bone registers 175°F (see page 106), about 30 minutes longer.

Transfer the chicken, breast side up, to a carving board (a cutting board with a groove to capture poultry juices) and let rest for 10–20 minutes, tenting with aluminum foil if needed to keep it warm. Carve the chicken into serving pieces and serve on warmed plates, asking your guests whether they prefer dark meat (from the leg and thigh), white meat (from the breast), or a combination.

Roasted Cornish Hens

For an intimate Thanksgiving celebration, consider these individual birds flavored with a tangy orange and onion sauce. The ratio of meat to bone is small, so plan to serve 1 hen per person.

MAKES 4 SERVINGS

About 30 minutes before roasting, remove the hens from the refrigerator. Pull out and discard the yellow pads of fat from both sides of the body cavity. Pat the hens dry with paper towels.

Position a rack in the center of the oven and preheat it to 425°F.

Using a vegetable peeler, remove the zest from 1 orange in ½-inch strips. Working with 1 orange at a time, cut a slice off the top and bottom to reveal the flesh. Stand the fruit upright. Using a sharp knife, thickly slice away the peel and pith, cutting downward and following the natural contour of the fruit. Holding the fruit over a bowl, cut along either side of each section of flesh, freeing it from its membrane and dropping the flesh into the bowl. Repeat with the remaining oranges. Coarsely chop the flesh and set aside. Place 3 or 4 strips of zest and 2 garlic clove halves inside each hen. Truss the hens (see page 105), if desired. Place on a plate, brush or rub with oil, season with salt and pepper, cover lightly with plastic wrap, and refrigerate for 3–4 hours.

Add the sliced onions to the reserved orange pieces and toss with the 1½ tablespoons olive oil. Transfer to the prepared pan and make a bed in the bottom of the pan. Place the hens, breast sides up, on the onions and oranges. Roast the hens until a thermometer inserted into the thickest part of the hen breasts away from the bone registers 160°F, 50–60 minutes.

Transfer the hens to a platter. Let rest for 10 minutes. Using a slotted spoon, divide the onion-orange mixture evenly among warmed individual plates, top each with a hen, and serve right away.

Cornish hens, 4, about 1½ pounds each

Oranges, 4

Garlic cloves, 4, cut in half

Extra-virgin olive oil for coating, plus 1½ tablespoons

Salt and freshly ground pepper

Sweet onions such as Vidalia or Maui, 4, cut into slices ¼ inch thick

Vegetable Potpie

Crusty, cheese-streaked biscuits provide a golden brown topping on this hearty, old-fashioned potpie. If you like, make individual servings in 1½-cup ovenproof bowls. Serve extra biscuits alongside.

MAKES ABOUT 12 SERVINGS

Preheat the oven to 425°F. Line 2 rimmed baking sheets with parchment paper.

Cut the potato, sweet potato, squash, carrots, parsnip, and onion into ¾-inch pieces and place in a large bowl with the mushrooms. Drizzle with the olive oil, sprinkle with salt and pepper, and toss to coat. Spread the vegetables in a single layer on the prepared pans. Roast, stirring once or twice, until lightly golden, about 25 minutes. Transfer the vegetables to a shallow 2½-quart baking dish. Mix in the beans.

Dissolve the cornstarch in 2 tablespoons water. In a saucepan over high heat, combine the broth, sage, thyme, garlic, and pepper to taste and bring to a boil over high heat. Stir in the cornstarch mixture, reduce the heat to low, and simmer until slightly thickened, about 2 minutes. Pour over the vegetables.

Top the filling with the unbaked biscuit dough rounds. (Bake any extra biscuit dough alongside the potpie on an ungreased baking pan, if you like.)

Bake the potpie until the biscuits are golden brown and the filling is bubbling, 18–20 minutes. Serve right away.

Yukon gold potato, 1, peeled

Sweet potato, 1, peeled

Butternut squash, ¾-pound, peeled and seeded

Carrots, 2, peeled

Parsnip, 1, peeled

Yellow onion, 1

Portobello mushrooms, ½ pound, brushed clean and cut into thick strips

Olive oil, 2 tablespoons

Salt and freshly ground pepper

Canned cannellini beans, 1 cup, rinsed and drained

Cornstarch, 2 tablespoons

Reduced-sodium vegetable broth, 2½ cups

Fresh sage, 2 teaspoons minced

Fresh thyme, 2 teaspoons minced

Garlic cloves, 2, minced

Dough for Classic Biscuits (page 85), made with cheddar cheese, cut into rounds

Giblet Gravy

Giblet gravy is a classic way to enhance the flavor of roasted poultry at your Thanksgiving dinner. Take care not to use the liver of the bird, as it will impart a bitter taste to your gravy.

MAKES 12–15 SERVINGS

Quick Turkey Stock, 7 cups (page 31), or 7 cups high-quality, reduced-sodium chicken stock

Reserved neck, heart, and gizzard

Cornstarch, ¼ cup

Salt and freshly ground pepper

Place the roasting pan used to roast the bird, with any pan juices and vegetables, over 2 burners and turn the heat to medium-high. Add all but ¼ cup of the stock to the pan and bring to a brisk simmer. Stir to deglaze the pan, scraping up the browned bits from the bottom, about 5 minutes.

Pour the contents of the pan through a sieve set over a large bowl, pressing hard on the vegetables with the back of a large spoon to extract all the liquid; discard the solids. Spoon off as much of the fat from the liquid as possible, or pour the liquid through a fat separator. Transfer the juices to a wide saucepan. Place over medium-high heat and simmer briskly for 5 minutes.

Finely chop the neck, heart, and gizzard and add the pieces to the saucepan. Reduce the heat to low. In a small bowl, stir together the remaining ¼ cup stock with the cornstarch to make a paste. Gradually stir the paste into the simmering gravy. Cook until the gravy thickens, 3–4 minutes. Season to taste with salt and pepper.

Pour the gravy into a warmed sauceboat or bowl with a ladle, and serve warm.

Herbed Citrus Gravy

The addition of fresh lemon juice, lemon zest, and parsley brighten the flavor of this gravy. Vary the herbs according to your preference; thyme, sage, and tarragon, or a combination, also work well.

MAKES 12–15 SERVINGS

Place the roasting pan used to roast the bird, with any pan juices and vegetables, over 2 burners and turn the heat to medium-high. Add all but $\frac{1}{4}$ cup of the stock to the pan and bring to a brisk simmer. Stir to deglaze the pan, scraping up the browned bits from the bottom, about 5 minutes.

Pour the contents of the pan through a sieve set over a large bowl, pressing hard on the vegetables with the back of a large spoon to extract all the liquid; discard the solids. Spoon off as much of the fat from the liquid as possible, or pour the liquid through a fat separator. Transfer the juices to a wide saucepan. Place over medium-high heat and simmer briskly for 5 minutes.

In a small bowl, stir together the remaining $\frac{1}{4}$ cup stock with the cornstarch to make a paste. Gradually stir the paste into the simmering gravy, then add the parsley, lemon juice, and the lemon zest. Cook until the gravy thickens, 3–4 minutes. Season to taste with salt and pepper.

Pour the gravy into a warmed sauceboat or bowl with a ladle, and serve warm.

Quick Turkey Stock, 7 cups (page 31), or 7 cups high-quality, reduced-sodium chicken stock

Cornstarch, $\frac{1}{4}$ cup

Fresh flat-leaf parsley, $\frac{1}{3}$ cup minced

Fresh lemon juice, 1 tablespoon

Lemon zest, 1 tablespoon minced

Salt and freshly ground pepper

Vegetables & Fruits

Maple-Glazed Acorn Squash

Acorn squash, with its attractive shape, slices beautifully into scalloped rings. For a lighter, more golden glaze, substitute honey for the maple syrup or use only butter without any added sweetener.

MAKES 4 SERVINGS

Preheat the oven to 400°F. Oil a rimmed baking sheet.

Trim the ends from each squash and cut crosswise into slices $\frac{1}{2}$ inch thick. Using a biscuit cutter slightly larger than the seeded center of each slice, cut out the seeds, leaving a neat circle in the center. Season the slices generously on both sides with the salt and pepper and arrange them in a single layer on the prepared pan. Roast the squash slices for about 10 minutes.

Meanwhile, in a small saucepan, melt the butter. Stir in the maple syrup, chopped thyme, and orange zest and remove from the heat.

When the squash slices have roasted for about 10 minutes, remove the pan from the oven and brush the tops of the slices evenly with the butter mixture. Sprinkle evenly with the cranberries. Continue to roast the squash slices until glazed, browned, and tender when pierced with a fork, 10–15 minutes longer.

Remove the pan from the oven and transfer the squash rings to a platter. Garnish with the thyme sprigs and serve at once.

Canola oil for greasing

Acorn squashes, 2

Salt and freshly ground pepper

Unsalted butter, 1½ tablespoons

Maple syrup, 2 tablespoons

Fresh thyme, 1 tablespoon chopped, plus sprigs for garnish

Grated orange zest, 2 teaspoons

Dried cranberries, 2 tablespoons chopped

Broccoli Rabe with Parmesan

Parmesan shavings give these healthy greens, a favorite of Italian cooks, a flavor boost. Rinse and trim the broccoli rabe early in the day, then store in the refrigerator until you are ready to roast it.

MAKES 8–10 SERVINGS

Broccoli rabe, 2½ pounds

Extra-virgin olive oil,
2 tablespoons

Balsamic vinegar,
1 tablespoon

Salt and freshly ground pepper

Parmigiano-Reggiano cheese, 1½-ounce wedge

Preheat the oven to 400°F. Line a rimmed baking sheet with parchment paper.

Trim off and discard 1 inch from the stem ends of the broccoli rabe and place the greens in a bowl. Add the oil and vinegar and toss to coat. Spread the broccoli rabe evenly on the prepared pan.

Roast until tender-crisp, 20–25 minutes, stirring once halfway through roasting. Remove from the oven, season to taste with salt and pepper, and transfer to a warmed platter. Using a vegetable peeler, shave the cheese over the top. Serve right away.

Creamed Pearl Onions

Small, sweet pearl onions bound in a rich cream sauce are traditional on the holiday table. Cutting a tiny cross into the root end of each onion prevents the onions from "telescoping" during cooking.

MAKES 6 SERVINGS

Bring a saucepan three-fourths full of water to a boil. Add the onions, blanch for 2 minutes, drain, and immerse in cold water to cool. Trim the root ends, slip off the skins, then cut a small cross in the root end of each onion. Return the onions to the pan, add water just to cover, bring to a boil, reduce the heat to low, cover, and simmer gently until tender, 15–20 minutes.

Meanwhile, in a small saucepan over medium heat, melt the butter. Whisk in the flour and cook, stirring, for about 1 minute. Gradually whisk in the hot milk and cook, stirring constantly, until smooth and thickened, 2–3 minutes. Add the nutmeg and season to taste with salt and white pepper.

Drain the onions well and return them to the pan. Pour the sauce over the onions, stir to coat the onions well, and transfer the mixture to a warmed serving dish. Sprinkle with the parsley and serve right away.

Pearl onions or other small white boiling onions, about 1½ pounds

Unsalted butter, 2 tablespoons

All-purpose flour, 2 tablespoons

Whole milk, 1¼ cups, heated

Freshly grated nutmeg, ¼ teaspoon

Salt and freshly ground white pepper

Fresh flat-leaf parsley, 2 tablespoons minced

Roasted Root Vegetables

Roasting caramelizes the sugars in root vegetables, making for a naturally sweet side dish. Any leftover vegetables are also excellent served as a salad at room temperature the next day.

MAKES 6–8 SERVINGS

Butternut squash, 1, about 1 pound, peeled, seeded, and cut into 2-inch pieces

Yukon gold potatoes, 3, unpeeled, cut into 2-inch wedges

Rutabaga, 1, peeled and cut into 2-inch pieces

Large red onion, 1, cut into ½-inch wedges

Slender carrots, 3, peeled and cut into 1½-inch lengths

Turnips, 2, peeled and cut into ½-inch wedges

Olive oil, 2 tablespoons

Balsamic vinegar, 1 tablespoon

Herbes de Provence, 1 teaspoon

Salt and freshly ground pepper

Preheat the oven to 400°F. Line 2 rimmed baking sheets with parchment paper.

In a large bowl, combine the squash, potatoes, rutabaga, onion, carrots, and turnips. Drizzle with the oil and vinegar, sprinkle with the herbes de Provence and salt and pepper to taste, and toss to coat. Spread the vegetables in a single layer on the prepared pans.

Roast the vegetables for 20 minutes. Stir and turn the vegetables, then continue to roast, stirring once or twice, until tender when pierced with a sharp knife, 25–35 minutes longer.

Adjust the seasonings, transfer to a warmed platter, and serve right away.

Sautéed Green Beans

Green beans are always a crowd-pleaser. Here, a quick sauté and a scattering of butter-toasted pecans make a winning dish. You can trim the beans in the morning, so they are ready to cook at dinner time.

MAKES 4–6 SERVINGS

Salt and freshly ground pepper

Young, slender green beans or haricots verts, about 1½ pounds, ends trimmed

Olive oil, 2 tablespoons

Fresh tarragon, 2 teaspoons minced, or ½ teaspoon dried tarragon

Unsalted butter, 1 tablespoon

Pecan halves, 6 tablespoons

Bring a saucepan three-fourths full of water to a boil over high heat, season with salt, add the beans, and cook until tender-crisp, 4–5 minutes. Drain and immediately immerse in cold water to halt the cooking. Drain again and pat dry. Return the beans to the pan and place over medium heat. Drizzle in the olive oil and sauté the beans until coated with the oil. Remove from the heat and sprinkle with the tarragon.

In a small frying pan over medium heat, melt the butter. Add the pecans and sauté until lightly browned, 2–3 minutes. Remove from the heat.

Transfer the beans to a warmed serving bowl and scatter the pecans over the top. Season to taste with salt and pepper and serve right away.

Red Onion Marmalade

This tart onion relish can be prepared up to 3 days in advance of serving. Let cool, cover tightly, and refrigerate, rewarming it over low heat for a few minutes just before serving.

MAKES 8–10 SERVINGS

In a very large frying pan over medium heat, melt half of the butter. Add half of the onions and 1 teaspoon salt, cover, and cook, stirring occasionally, until the onions are tender and have rendered some of their liquid, about 15 minutes. Transfer to a bowl. Repeat with the remaining butter, onions, and another 1 teaspoon salt.

Return the first batch of onions and any juices from their bowl to the frying pan with the second batch of onions. Stir in the brown sugar and cassis, and then add the vinegar. Cook over low heat, stirring and tossing frequently, until the onion juices have evaporated, about 30 minutes. Continue to cook uncovered, stirring occasionally, until the onions are tender and lightly browned, another 20–30 minutes.

Add the thyme and season to taste with salt and pepper. Serve warm.

Unsalted butter, ½ cup

Large red onions, 10, halved and thinly sliced

Salt and freshly ground pepper

Light brown sugar, ⅓ cup firmly packed

Crème de cassis, ⅓ cup

Red wine vinegar, ⅓ cup

Fresh thyme, 1 tablespoon minced, or 1½ teaspoons dried thyme

Brussels Sprouts with Bacon

Crisp, smoky bacon and mellow vinegar boost the flavor of Brussels sprouts. To save time, cook the sprouts 1 day in advance, chill in ice water, drain, and refrigerate. Then, glaze just before serving.

MAKES 8 SERVINGS

Cut a shallow cross in the stem end of each Brussels sprout. Bring a large saucepan three-fourths full of salted water to a boil, add the Brussels sprouts, and cook until tender, 6–8 minutes. Drain well, transfer to a warmed bowl, and keep warm while you cook the bacon.

In a large frying pan over medium-high heat, sauté the bacon pieces until crisp, 7–8 minutes. Using a slotted spoon, transfer to paper towels to drain. Pour off all but 2 tablespoons of the bacon fat and return the pan to medium-high heat. Add the vinegar to the reserved bacon fat in the pan and cook, stirring, until reduced to a glaze, 5–7 minutes.

Scatter the bacon pieces over the Brussels sprouts, and then spoon the glaze over the top. Toss lightly and season with salt and pepper. Serve right away.

Brussels sprouts, about 2½ pounds, stems trimmed and discolored leaves discarded

Salt and freshly ground pepper

Thick-cut bacon, 8 slices, diced

Balsamic vinegar, ⅓ cup

Citrus & Mint Compote

Mixing blood oranges with deep, tangy crème de cassis and fresh mint is an inspired way to add fruit to your Thanksgiving menu. Serve this as an alternative to traditional cranberry sauce.

MAKES 8–10 SERVINGS

Large blood oranges or navel oranges, 12

Crème de cassis, ¼ cup

Fresh lemon juice, 2 tablespoons

Fresh mint, 3 tablespoons minced, plus mint sprigs for garnish

Orange zest, 1 tablespoon freshly grated

Pomegranate seeds for garnish (optional)

Working with 1 orange at a time, cut a slice off the top and bottom to reveal the flesh. Stand the fruit upright. Using a sharp knife, thickly slice away the peel and pith, cutting downward and following the natural contour of the fruit. Holding the fruit over a bowl, cut along either side of each section of flesh, freeing it from its membrane and dropping the flesh into the bowl. Repeat this process with the remaining oranges.

Pour the cassis and lemon juice over the oranges and stir to blend. Cover and refrigerate for 30–60 minutes.

To serve, transfer the oranges to a serving dish and sprinkle with the minced mint, orange zest, and the pomegranate seeds, if using. Garnish with mint sprigs and serve.

Cranberry-Apple Chutney

Fresh ginger lends a spicy flavor to this tangy chutney. If you prefer a sweeter taste, increase the sugar by 1–2 tablespoons. Make the chutney 1–2 days in advance to allow the flavors to mellow.

MAKES 6 SERVINGS

Peel and core the apple, then it into quarters and then into 1-inch chunks.

In a food processor, combine the apple, cranberries, sugar, and ginger and process until finely minced. Transfer to an airtight container and refrigerate, tightly covered, until ready to serve.

Granny Smith apple, 1

Fresh cranberries, 3 cups

Sugar, ¾ cup

Fresh ginger, peeled and cut into two ⅛-inch slices

Classic Cranberry Sauce

Fresh cranberry sauce is easy to make and has a better flavor than canned sauce. If you like, add 2 teaspoons freshly grated orange or lemon zest, or 1 peeled, cored, and diced apple.

MAKES 6 SERVINGS

Water, 1 cup

Sugar, 1 cup

Fresh cranberries, 3 cups

In a saucepan, combine the water and sugar and bring to a boil over medium-high heat, stirring to dissolve the sugar. Add the cranberries, reduce the heat to low, and simmer just until all the cranberries pop, about 10 minutes.

Remove from the heat, skim off the foam with a large spoon, and let the sauce cool to room temperature. (The sauce will keep in an airtight container in the refrigerator for up to 3 days.) Serve at room temperature or chill in the refrigerator and serve cold.

Potatoes & Stuffings

Sour Cream Mashed Potatoes

A quick sauté sweetens the green onions in this creamy potato side dish. Don't over-work the potatoes when mashing them, or they will lose their creamy texture and become gluey.

MAKES 6–8 SERVINGS

In a large saucepan, combine the potatoes with salted water to cover generously. Bring to a boil over medium heat, cover, and simmer, stirring once or twice, until the potatoes are tender when pierced with a fork, about 25–30 minutes.

Just before the potatoes are ready, in a small frying pan over low heat, melt 1 tablespoon of the butter. Add the green onions and cook just until they turn opaque, 1–2 minutes. Remove from the heat.

Drain the potatoes, reserving about 1 cup of the cooking liquid. Return the potatoes to the pan over low heat. Using a potato masher, mash the potatoes. Using a wooden spoon, slowly stir in the hot milk, the remaining 2 tablespoons butter, the sour cream, and the green onions, and continue to stir until light and fluffy. If the potatoes seem a little dry, stir in some of the reserved cooking liquid. Season to taste with salt and pepper.

Transfer the potatoes to a warmed serving dish and serve right away.

Yukon gold potatoes or russet potatoes, about 2½ pounds, peeled and cut into large chunks

Salt and freshly ground pepper

Unsalted butter, 3 tablespoons

Green onions, ½ cup minced, including tender green tops

Whole milk, ½ cup, heated

Sour cream, ½ cup

Buttermilk Mashed Potatoes

Both Yukon gold and russet potatoes are good candidates for mashing, especially when combined with the zesty tang of buttermilk. Minced chives lend visual appeal and heighten the flavor.

MAKES 8 SERVINGS

Yukon gold potatoes
or russet potatoes, about 2½ pounds, peeled and cut into large chunks

Salt and freshly ground pepper

Whole milk, ⅔ cup

Unsalted butter, 6 tablespoons

Buttermilk, ⅔ cup

Fresh chives, ¼ cup snipped

In a large saucepan, combine the potatoes with salted water to cover generously. Bring to a boil over medium heat, cover, and simmer, stirring once or twice, until the potatoes are very tender when pierced with a fork, 25–30 minutes.

Just before the potatoes are ready, in a small saucepan over medium heat, combine the milk, butter, and buttermilk and heat until the butter has melted and the milk is hot.

Drain the potatoes, reserving about 1 cup of the cooking liquid. Return the potatoes to the pan over low heat. Using a potato masher, mash the potatoes. Using a wooden spoon, slowly stir in the hot milk mixture. Slowly stir in the chives and ¼ teaspoon salt, and continue to stir until light and fluffy. If the potatoes seem a little dry, stir in some of the reserved cooking liquid. Season to taste with salt and pepper.

Transfer the potatoes to a warmed serving bowl and serve right away.

Potato & Celery Root Purée

The intriguing taste of celery root adds a new twist to traditional mashed potatoes. The grated fresh horseradish will contribute a spicy bite, so adjust the amount according to your taste.

MAKES 6–8 SERVINGS

In a large saucepan over high heat, combine 2 cups water with the milk and ½ teaspoon salt and bring to a boil. Add the celery root, potatoes, and onion and bring back to a boil. Reduce the heat to low, cover partially, and simmer until the vegetables are tender, 25–30 minutes. Drain, reserving 1 cup of the cooking liquid.

In a food processor, combine the hot cooked vegetables and the butter and process until smooth. If the purée is too stiff, add the reserved liquid as needed to loosen it. Add the horseradish and salt to taste.

Transfer the purée to a warmed serving bowl, sprinkle with the chives, and serve right away.

Whole milk, 2 cups

Kosher salt

Large celery root, 1, peeled and cut into 2-inch cubes

Large russet potatoes, 2, peeled and cut into 2-inch cubes

Small yellow onion, 1, quartered

Unsalted butter, 4 tablespoons

Fresh horseradish, about 1 tablespoon grated

Fresh chives, 1 tablespoon snipped

Chipotle–Sweet Potato Gratin

Chipotle chiles in adobo are smoke-dried jalapeños packed in a spicy tomato-and-vinegar sauce. They add a lively spark of flavor to autumn's sweet potatoes. Adjust the chipotles to suit your taste.

MAKES 6–8 SERVINGS

Sweet potatoes or garnet yams, 4 or 5

Unsalted butter, 3 tablespoons

Canned chipotle chile in adobo, 1 teaspoon finely chopped

Light brown sugar, 6 tablespoons firmly packed

Heavy cream, 3/4 cup

Salt and freshly ground pepper

Preheat the oven to 400°F. Prick each sweet potato in several spots with a fork and place on a rimmed baking sheet. Bake until tender when pierced with a knife, 35–45 minutes. Transfer to a wire rack and let cool to room temperature, then peel and slice thickly. Reduce the oven temperature to 375°F.

Butter a 9-inch square baking dish. Arrange the sweet potato slices in the dish, overlapping them. In a small saucepan over medium heat, combine the butter, chile, sugar, and cream and heat, stirring, until blended. Pour evenly over the potatoes. Sprinkle the gratin with salt and pepper. (You can assemble the gratin to this point up to 1 day in advance and store it, tightly covered with plastic wrap, in the refrigerator. Increase the baking time to about 30 minutes.)

Bake the gratin until heated through, about 15 minutes. Serve right away.

Rice Pilaf with Dried Fruit

To make a brown rice version of this pilaf, increase the broth to 2½ cups and simmer for 45 minutes or bake for about 1 hour and 10 minutes. You can also vary the nuts and dried fruits, if you like.

MAKES 4 SERVINGS

Preheat the oven to 350°F. Spread the almonds on a small, shallow pan and toast, stirring once or twice to prevent scorching, until fragrant and slightly darkened, 8–10 minutes. Pour onto a plate to cool.

In a saucepan over medium heat, warm the olive oil. Add the onion and sauté until soft, 7–8 minutes. Add the rice and cook, stirring often, until opaque, 2–3 minutes. Add the broth, cranberries, thyme, and a pinch each of salt and pepper. Cover, reduce the heat to low, and cook until the liquid is absorbed and the rice is tender, about 20 minutes. Alternatively, transfer the mixture to a baking dish, place in a preheated 350°F oven, and cook until the liquid is absorbed and the rice is tender, 30–40 minutes.

If cooked on the stove top, transfer the rice to a warmed serving dish. If baked, serve directly from the baking dish. Sprinkle the toasted almonds over the top and serve right away.

Slivered blanched almonds, ⅓ cup

Olive oil or unsalted butter, 3 tablespoons

Yellow onion, 1¼ cups finely chopped

Long-grain white rice, 1 cup

Reduced-sodium chicken broth or beef broth, 2 cups, heated

Dried cranberries, currants, or golden raisins, ⅓ cup

Dried thyme, ½ teaspoon

Salt and freshly ground pepper

Sweet Potato Purée

Honey and fresh lemon juice deliver a balance of sweet and tart flavors in this easy-to-make side dish. If you like, you can prepare it up to 2 days in advance and reheat it just before serving.

MAKES 8 SERVINGS

Large sweet potatoes,
4 or 5

Unsalted butter,
4 tablespoons

Honey, ¼ cup

Fresh lemon juice,
3 tablespoons

Apple juice, ½ cup, heated

Salt and freshly ground pepper

Preheat the oven to 400°F. Prick each sweet potato in several spots with a fork and place on a rimmed baking sheet. Bake until tender when pierced with a knife, 50–60 minutes. Let cool for about 5 minutes, or just until they can be handled, and then halve lengthwise and scoop out the flesh into a bowl.

Meanwhile, in a small saucepan over medium heat, warm together the butter, honey, and lemon juice until hot. Using a potato masher, mash the potatoes. Add ⅓ cup of the apple juice, the honey mixture, and salt and pepper to taste. Still using the masher, mix lightly until smooth. If the purée isn't smooth, mix in additional apple juice as needed.

Spoon the purée into a warmed serving dish and serve right away. (You can make this purée up to 2 days in advance. To serve it, transfer the purée to a small baking dish and reheat it in a 350°F oven for 15–20 minutes.)

Sausage & Apricot Stuffing

Spicy sausage counters the sweet apricots in this hearty recipe. You can toast the bread and cook the sausage, onions, and celery 1 day in advance. Combine the ingredients just before stuffing or baking.

MAKES STUFFING FOR A 12-POUND TURKEY; 10–12 SERVINGS

In a large frying pan over medium heat, cook the sausages, breaking up the clumps with a wooden spoon and stirring occasionally, until lightly browned, about 10 minutes. Transfer to a large bowl and discard the fat in the pan.

Return the pan to low heat and add the oil. Add the onions and celery and cook, stirring occasionally, until soft, 7–8 minutes. Add to the bowl with the sausage. Add the bread cubes, apricots, and parsley and toss to mix. Season with the sage, thyme, nutmeg, and salt and pepper to taste and toss again. Moisten with the broth, $1/2$ cup at a time, tossing well after each addition, until the ingredients are combined and the mixture is moist throughout but not soggy.

Allow the stuffing to cool to room temperature. Then, following the directions on page 42, stuff two-thirds of the stuffing into the bird. Put the rest of the stuffing into a small, buttered baking dish and cover tightly with aluminum foil. During the last hour the turkey is roasting, bake the extra stuffing in the oven alongside the turkey for 30 minutes. Uncover and continue to bake until heated through and lightly browned and crisp on top, 20–30 minutes longer. (Alternatively, if you do not want to stuff the turkey, transfer the stuffing—now called dressing—to a buttered 4-quart baking dish and bake according to the above instructions.)

Using a large spoon, transfer the stuffing from the turkey cavity to a warmed serving dish. Keep warm until ready to serve.

Well-spiced pork sausages or turkey sausages, 1 pound, casings removed and meat broken into clumps

Canola oil, 2 tablespoons

Large yellow onions, 2, finely chopped

Celery stalks, 2, with some leaves, finely chopped

Country-style bread, 1 loaf, about 1 pound, cut into $1/2$-inch cubes with or without crusts (10 cups)

Dried apricots, 1 cup minced

Fresh flat-leaf parsley, $1/3$ cup minced

Dried sage, 1 teaspoon

Dried thyme, $1^{1}/2$ teaspoons

Freshly grated nutmeg, $1/2$ teaspoon

Salt and freshly ground pepper

Reduced-sodium chicken broth, $1^{1}/2$–2 cups

Apple & Cranberry Stuffing

The sweet-tart character of the apples and tang of the cranberries deliver big flavor to this quick-to-assemble stuffing. You can toast the bread cubes and cook the onions and celery 1 day in advance.

MAKES STUFFING FOR A 12-POUND TURKEY; 10–12 SERVINGS

Preheat the oven to 350°F. Spread the bread on 2 rimmed baking sheets and toast in the oven, stirring once or twice, until golden and dry, 15–20 minutes. Remove from the oven. In a large frying pan over medium heat, melt 2 tablespoons of the butter. Add the onions and celery and sauté until soft, about 10 minutes. Transfer to a large bowl. Return the pan to medium heat and add 1 tablespoon of the butter. Add the apples and sauté until glazed and browned, about 5 minutes. Add the apples to the onion mixture and season with sage, thyme, nutmeg, and salt and pepper to taste. Return the pan to medium heat and melt the remaining 5 tablespoons butter. Add the bread cubes, cranberries, and parsley and toss to coat with the butter. Add the bread mixture to the bowl and toss. Moisten with the broth, 1/2 cup at a time, tossing well after each addition, until the ingredients are combined and the mixture is moist throughout but not soggy.

Allow the stuffing to cool to room temperature. Then, following the directions on page 42, stuff two-thirds of the stuffing into the bird. Put the rest of the stuffing into a small, buttered baking dish and cover tightly with aluminum foil. During the last hour the turkey is roasting, bake the extra stuffing in the oven alongside the turkey for 30 minutes. Uncover and continue to bake until heated through and lightly browned and crisp on top, 20–30 minutes longer. (Alternatively, if you do not want to stuff the turkey, transfer the stuffing—now called dressing—to a buttered 4-quart baking dish and bake according to the above instructions.)

Using a large spoon, transfer the stuffing from the turkey cavity to a warmed serving dish. Keep warm until ready to serve.

Country-style bread, 1 loaf, about 1 pound, cut into 1/2-inch cubes with or without crusts (10 cups)

Unsalted butter, 8 tablespoons

Large yellow onions, 2, finely chopped

Celery stalks, 2, with some leaves, finely chopped

Large Granny Smith apples, 2, cored and diced

Fresh sage, 2 tablespoons chopped, or 1 teaspoon dried sage

Dried thyme, 1 teaspoon

Freshly grated nutmeg, 1/2 teaspoon

Salt and freshly ground pepper

Dried cranberries, 1 cup

Fresh flat-leaf parsley, 1/3 cup minced

Reduced-sodium chicken broth, 1 1/2–2 cups, heated

Cornbread Stuffing with Bacon

This flavorful cornbread stuffing offers a nice nutty flavor accented by the addition of salty, smoky bacon. Cook the onions slowly so they develop a caramel flavor without overbrowning.

MAKES STUFFING FOR A 12-POUND TURKEY; 10–12 SERVINGS

Thick-cut bacon, 8 slices

Large yellow onions, 2, coarsely chopped

Celery stalks, 2, with some leaves, finely chopped

Cornbread stuffing mix, 10 cups

Fresh flat-leaf parsley, 1/3 cup minced

Dried sage, 1 teaspoon

Herbes de Provence, 2 teaspoons

Salt and freshly ground pepper

Reduced-sodium chicken broth, 1 1/2–2 cups, heated

In a large frying pan over medium heat, cook the bacon until crisp, about 8 minutes. Using a slotted spoon, transfer the bacon to paper towels to drain and cool slightly. Place the bacon in a large bowl.

Drain off all but 2 tablespoons of the bacon fat from the pan and return to low heat. Add the onions to the pan and cook over low heat, stirring occasionally, until golden, about 7 minutes. Add the celery to the onions and cook for an additional 3–4 minutes. Add the onion mixture, stuffing mix, parsley, sage, and herbes de Provence to the bowl with the bacon and toss well. Season to taste with salt and pepper. Moisten with the broth, 1/2 cup at a time, tossing well after each addition, until the ingredients are combined and the mixture is moist throughout but not soggy.

Allow the stuffing to cool to room temperature. Then, following the directions on page 42, stuff two-thirds of the stuffing into the bird. Put the rest of the stuffing into a small, buttered baking dish and cover tightly with aluminum foil. During the last hour the turkey is roasting, bake the extra stuffing in the oven alongside the turkey for 30 minutes. Uncover and continue to bake until heated through and lightly browned and crisp on top, 20–30 minutes longer. (Alternatively, if you do not want to stuff the turkey, transfer the stuffing—now called dressing—to a buttered 4-quart baking dish and bake according to the above instructions.)

Using a large spoon, transfer the stuffing from the turkey cavity to a warmed serving dish. Keep warm until ready to serve.

Classic Biscuits

For tender, flaky biscuits, it is important to have a light touch. Biscuits, and quick breads in general, benefit from minimal stirring. Sharp cheddar cheese added to the batter makes a flavorful variation.

Position a rack in the middle of the oven, and preheat to 425°F. Line a baking sheet with parchment paper.

In a large bowl, stir together the flour, baking powder, salt, and Cheddar, if desired. Using a pastry blender or 2 knives, cut in the butter until the mixture forms coarse crumbs. Slowly pour in the milk and stir and toss with a fork just until the mixture is evenly moistened.

Turn out the dough on a lightly floured work surface and press together. Knead a few times, then pat into a ball and flatten into a disk. Roll out into a round about ¾ inch thick. Using a 3-inch round cutter, cut out as many rounds as possible. Gather the scraps and repeat rolling out and cutting biscuit rounds until no scraps remain.

Place the biscuit rounds on the baking sheets and bake until golden brown, about 18 minutes. Remove from the oven and let cool on a wire rack for 8–10 minutes before serving. Serve slightly warm.

All-purpose flour,
2 cups

Baking powder,
2½ teaspoons

Salt, ½ teaspoon

Cheddar cheese, ½ cup
shredded (optional)

Unsalted butter,
6 tablespoons, chilled and
cut into ½-inch pieces

Whole milk, ¾ cup

Desserts

Gingersnap Pumpkin Pie

The crunchy cookie crust makes an easy-to-assemble base for the creamy pumpkin filling. The pie can be made up to 1 day in advance. Serve with whipped cream flavored with Cognac, if you wish.

MAKES 8 SERVINGS

Preheat the oven to 350°F.

To make the crust, in a small bowl, stir together the gingersnap crumbs, granulated sugar, melted butter, and ginger until evenly moistened. Pat evenly into the bottom and up the sides of a 9-inch pie pan. Bake just until set, about 5 minutes. Let cool completely on a rack.

To make the filling, in a large bowl, whisk the eggs until blended. Whisk in the brown sugar, cinnamon, ginger, cloves, nutmeg, and salt until well mixed. Stir in the pumpkin and half-and-half until blended. Pour into the crust.

Bake the pie until the filling is set, 45–50 minutes. Let cool completely on a rack. Cut into wedges, top each wedge with whipped cream, and serve.

GINGERSNAP CRUST

Crushed gingersnaps, 1½ cups

Granulated sugar, 3 tablespoons

Unsalted butter, 6 tablespoons, melted

Ground ginger, ½ teaspoon

FILLING

Large eggs, 3

Light brown sugar, ¾ cup firmly packed

Ground cinnamon, ½ teaspoon

Ground ginger, ½ teaspoon

Ground cloves, ¼ teaspoon

Freshly grated nutmeg, ¼ teaspoon

Salt, ½ teaspoon

Canned pumpkin purée, 1⅔ cups

Half-and-half or heavy cream, 1½ cups

Whipped cream for serving

Chocolate-Cranberry Torte

The unique combination of rich, dark chocolate with tart dried cranberries is sure to become a new favorite. Finish the cake with dusting of confectioners' sugar and serve it with vanilla bean ice cream.

MAKES 12 SERVINGS

Almonds or hazelnuts, or a combination, ¾ cup

Bittersweet chocolate or semisweet chocolate, 8 ounces, chopped

Unsalted butter, ¾ cup

Granulated sugar, ¾ cup

Vanilla extract, 1 teaspoon

Large eggs, 3

All-purpose flour, ⅔ cup

Dried cranberries, 1⅓ cups

Confectioners' sugar for dusting

Preheat the oven to 350°F. Line the bottom of a 9-inch springform pan with parchment paper.

Spread the nuts on a small, shallow pan and toast until slightly darkened and fragrant, 8–10 minutes. (If using hazelnuts, pour the warm nuts onto paper towels and rub between your palms to remove most of their papery skins.) Let the nuts cool, then transfer to a food processor and pulse until finely ground.

Put the chocolate in a heatproof bowl and place over (but not touching) barely simmering water in a saucepan. Heat, stirring occasionally, just until melted, then remove from the heat and let cool.

In a large bowl, using a mixer on medium speed, beat the butter until light. Add the sugar and vanilla and beat until fluffy, about 2 minutes. Add the eggs one at a time, beating well after each addition. With the mixer on low speed, add the chocolate and mix until smooth. Add the flour and ground nuts and mix just until blended. Using a rubber spatula, fold in 1 cup of the cranberries. Pour the batter into the prepared pan and smooth the surface. Sprinkle the remaining ⅓ cup cranberries evenly on top. Bake the torte until a toothpick inserted in the center comes out clean, about 35 minutes. Let cool on a rack for 30 minutes.

Using a knife, loosen the torte from the pan sides. Invert a serving plate on the pan and, holding both, invert them together to release the torte. Release and remove the pan sides, lift off the pan bottom, and peel off the parchment. Let cool to room temperature. Just before serving, using a fine-mesh sieve, dust the top of the cake with confectioners' sugar. Cut into wedges and serve.

Pecan Tartlets

This pastry is easy to shape, and both the pastry and the filling can be doubled or tripled for a crowd. You can bake the pastry shells 2 days ahead of time and store them, covered, at room temperature.

MAKES 4 TARTLETS

Preheat the oven to 400°F.

To make the pastry, in a food processor, combine the flour and granulated sugar and pulse a few times to mix. Add the butter and pulse until the mixture resembles fine crumbs. Add the egg yolk and pulse until blended. Add 3 tablespoons of the ice water and pulse just until the dough clings together, adding up to 1 tablespoon more water if needed.

Pinch off one-fourth of the dough and press it evenly onto the bottom and up the sides of a 4½-inch tartlet pan with a removable bottom. Repeat to line three more 4½-inch tartlet pans. Place the pans in the freezer for 10 minutes to firm up the pastry, then arrange them on a rimmed baking sheet. Line the shells with aluminum foil and use pie weights or dried beans to weight the shells. Bake the pastry shells until set but still pale, about 10 minutes. Remove from the oven. Reduce the oven temperature to 350°F.

In a large bowl, whisk together the eggs until light and fluffy. Add the brown sugar, corn syrup, melted butter, Cognac, salt, and vanilla and whisk until smooth. Stir in the nuts.

Divide the filling evenly among the pastry shells. Bake until the top is browned and the filling is set, 20–25 minutes. Let cool on a rack to room temperature, remove from the tartlet pans, and serve.

PASTRY

All-purpose flour, 1½ cups

Granulated sugar, 1 tablespoon

Unsalted butter, ¾ cup chilled, cut into ½-inch pieces

Large egg yolk, 1

Ice water, 3–4 tablespoons

FILLING

Large eggs, 3

Light brown sugar, 1 cup firmly packed

Dark corn syrup, ¾ cup

Unsalted butter, ⅓ cup, melted and slightly cooled

Cognac, 1 tablespoon

Salt, ¼ teaspoon

Vanilla extract, 1 teaspoon

Pecan pieces, 1¾ cups

Upside-Down Pumpkin Tart

This tart is reminiscent of a Tarte Tatin, traditionally made with apples. Tender golden-orange sugar pumpkin makes a festive autumn stand-in. If you like, top each serving with a dollop of crème fraîche.

MAKES 8 SERVINGS

Pastry (page 93)

Sugar pumpkin, 1, halved, seeded, peeled, and cut into slices ¾ inch thick and about 3 inches long (do not substitute a regular pumpkin)

Olive oil, 2 tablespoons

Unsalted butter, 6 tablespoons, at room temperature

Sugar, 1 cup

Ground cinnamon, 2 teaspoons

Ground ginger, ½ teaspoon

Preheat the oven to 400°F. Line a rimmed baking sheet with parchment paper.

Follow the instructions on page 93 to make the pastry. Gather the pastry into a ball, flatten into a disk, wrap with plastic, and refrigerate for at least 1 hour or for up to 1 day.

To make the filling, spread the pumpkin slices in a single layer on the baking sheet. Brush them on both sides with the oil. Bake, turning twice, until almost tender when pierced with a knife, about 30 minutes. Remove from the oven.

Spread the butter over the bottom of a heavy, nonstick 10-inch ovenproof frying pan. Sprinkle all but 1 tablespoon of the sugar over the butter. Place over medium-low heat until the sugar begins to melt, 4–5 minutes. Remove from the heat and arrange the pumpkin slices in the pan, placing them close together and covering the bottom completely. In a small bowl, stir together the reserved 1 tablespoon sugar, the cinnamon, and the ginger, and sprinkle evenly over the pumpkin.

On a floured work surface, roll the pastry into an 11-inch round. Drape the pastry around the rolling pin, position it over the pan, and unroll the pastry evenly over the pumpkin slices, tucking the edges into the pan. Bake until the crust is golden and the pumpkin is tender, about 20 minutes. Remove the pan from the oven and let cool for 1 minute.

Using a knife, loosen the crust from the pan sides. Invert a serving plate on the pan and, holding both, invert them together to release the tart onto the plate. Let cool slightly, cut into wedges, and serve warm.

Gingerbread with Brandy Sauce

This gingerbread cake is accompanied by a delectable brandy sauce. You can prepare both 2 days in advance and store them, tightly covered, at room temperature. Reheat in a 350°F oven before serving.

MAKES 10–12 SERVINGS

Preheat the oven to 375°F. Butter a 9-inch round cake pan or springform pan with 2-inch sides. Dust the pan with flour and tap out the excess.

In a large bowl, stir together the butter, honey, and molasses. Add the sour cream and egg and beat until smooth. In a medium bowl, stir together the flour, baking soda, ginger, mustard, allspice, and cinnamon. Add the dry ingredients to the butter mixture and stir until blended. Slowly pour into the prepared pan.

Bake the cake until a toothpick inserted in the center comes out clean, 30–35 minutes. Let cool on a rack for 5 minutes, then invert onto the rack, releasing the pan sides if using a springform pan, and turn right side up to cool.

While the cake is baking, make the brandy sauce. In a bowl, whisk the egg yolk until blended. Add the sugar and brandy and whisk until smooth. In another bowl, whisk the cream until soft peaks form. Fold the cream into the sugar mixture. Cover and refrigerate until serving, up to 2 days in advance.

Cut the warm cake into wedges and serve topped with the brandy sauce.

Unsalted butter, 1/3 cup, melted

Honey, 1/2 cup

Light molasses, 1/2 cup

Sour cream or plain yogurt, 1/2 cup

Large egg, 1

All-purpose flour, 2 cups

Baking soda, 1 1/2 teaspoons

Ground ginger, 1 teaspoon

Dry mustard, 1/2 teaspoon

Allspice, 1/2 teaspoon

Ground cinnamon, 1/2 teaspoon

BRANDY SAUCE

Large egg yolk, 1

Confectioners' sugar, 1 cup

Brandy, 1/4 cup

Heavy cream, 3/4 cup

Caramel Pots de Crème

This creamy dessert features an easy stove top caramel sauce blended with a custard and baked. Top each serving with a generous dollop of whipped cream and a sprinkle of cinnamon, if you like.

MAKES 6 SERVINGS

Sugar, 1 cup

Heavy cream, 1½ cups

Milk, 1½ cups

Egg yolks, 8

Crème fraîche for serving

Ground cinnamon for sprinkling

In a heavy saucepan over medium-high heat, combine the sugar with ⅓ cup water. Cover and bring to a boil. Uncover the pan and cook until the sugar turns golden amber in color and forms a caramel, 8–12 minutes. Be careful, as the caramel is very hot.

Combine the cream and milk in a large saucepan over medium-high heat and warm until small bubbles appear at the edges of the pan. Remove from the heat.

Preheat an oven to 325°F. Add ¼ cup cool water to the caramel and whisk vigorously until the bubbles subside. Pour the caramel into the hot cream mixture and whisk together until mixed. Let cool for about 10 minutes.

In a bowl, whisk the egg yolks until smooth. Slowly add the caramel mixture, stirring constantly until mixed. Strain through a fine-mesh sieve into a glass measuring cup.

Have ready a kettle full of boiling water. Pour the custard into six ⅔-cup ramekins. Place the ramekins in a baking pan and place the pan on the oven shelf. Carefully pour the boiling water into the baking pan to reach about 1 inch up the sides of the ramekins. Bake until the edges of the custards are set, 40–50 minutes. Remove the baking pan from the oven and transfer to a rack to cool for about 10 minutes.

Carefully remove the custards from the water bath and let cool. Refrigerate for several hours or for up to overnight until well chilled. Garnish each with a dollop of crème fraîche, sprinkle with the cinnamon, and serve chilled or at room temperature.

Menu Inspirations

Creating a Thanksgiving menu that accomodates the spirit of your celebration and the tastes of your guests can be a challenge. The best way to proceed is to select a combination of starters, main dishes, side dishes, and desserts that offer a variety of colors, flavors, and textures and vary in cooking time. Many families serve a mixture of traditional dishes and unique family favorites, but the menu varies little from year to year. For a fresh approach, try adding new recipes to your repertoire to inspire new traditions. Use these menus to plan your entire meal or mix and match them to customize your own.

Fête for Two

Roasted Onion Soup
page 17

Herb-Roasted Chicken
page 46

Sautéed Green Beans
page 60

Sweet Potato Purée
page 78

Purchased Pumpkin Pie

A holiday meal for two can be just as celebratory as a feast for many. Simply add a store-bought pumpkin pie or other dessert to this easy three-course meal.

WORK PLAN

TWO DAYS IN ADVANCE
❑ Shop for all recipe ingredients
❑ Purée and store the sweet potatoes

ONE DAY IN ADVANCE
❑ Prepare and store the soup
❑ Purchase the pie

THE DAY OF THE MEAL
❑ Roast the chicken
❑ Sauté the green beans

To counter the stress of a big gathering, arrange the dishes on a buffet instead of plating them individually. For details on setting up a buffet, turn to page 8.

WORK PLAN

THREE DAYS IN ADVANCE

☐ Shop for all ingredients

☐ Make and store the horseradish sauce

TWO DAYS IN ADVANCE

☐ Make and store the chutney

☐ Prepare and store the tartlet crusts

ONE DAY IN ADVANCE

☐ Soak the wood chips for the turkey

☐ Bake and store the tartlets

☐ Plan the buffet (select and prepare the table, serving dishes, and utensils)

THE DAY OF THE MEAL

☐ Roast and stuff the figs

☐ Bake the biscuits

☐ Smoke the turkey

☐ Make the potato purée

☐ Roast the broccoli rabe

☐ Assemble and dress the salad

Turkey Buffet

....

Stuffed Roasted Figs
page 16

Watercress, Endive & Apple Salad
page 22

Hickory-Smoked Turkey
page 37

Horseradish-Apple Sauce
page 39

Cranberry-Apple Chutney
page 65

Potato & Celery Root Purée
page 73

Classic Biscuits
page 85

Broccoli Rabe with Parmesan
page 56

Pecan Tartlets
page 93

Traditional Dinner

This classic approach to the holiday meal will showcase a variety of tried-and-true seasonal favorites and family traditions that all of your guests are sure to enjoy.

WORK PLAN

THREE DAYS IN ADVANCE

❏ Shop for all ingredients
❏ Make and store the cranberry sauce
❏ Mix and store the compound butter for the turkey

TWO DAYS IN ADVANCE

❏ Make and store the soup
❏ Prepare and store the pie crust

ONE DAY IN ADVANCE

❏ Ready the ingredients for the stuffing
❏ Cook and store the Brussels sprouts
❏ Bake and store the pumpkin pie

THE DAY OF THE MEAL

❏ Make the stuffing
❏ Stuff and roast the turkey
❏ Glaze and finish the Brussels sprouts
❏ Prepare the mashed potatoes
❏ Make the gravy

A vegetarian meal doesn't have to mean an unexciting meal. The wide array of flavors, textures, and colors presented here all add spark to this meatless feast.

WORK PLAN

THREE DAYS IN ADVANCE

❑ Shop for all ingredients

❑ Toast and store the nuts for the salad

❑ Bake and store the crostini

❑ Process and store the tapenade

TWO DAYS IN ADVANCE

❑ Make and store the chutney

ONE DAY IN ADVANCE

❑ Cook and store the beets and green beans

❑ Bake and chill the pots de créme

THE DAY OF THE MEAL

❑ Assemble the crostini and tapenade

❑ Prepare the acorn squash

❑ Bake the potpie

❑ Put together the citrus compote

❑ Make the mashed potatoes

❑ Assemble and dress the salad

Vegetarian Thanksgiving

....

Crostini with Tapenade
page 15

Beet & Green Bean Salad
page 25

Vegetable Potpie
page 49

Cranberry-Apple Chutney
page 65

Citrus & Mint Compote
page 64

Maple-Glazed Acorn Squash
page 55

*Sour Cream
Mashed Potatoes*
page 71

Caramel Pots de Créme
page 96

Ideas for Leftovers

While Thanksgiving Day is the main event, the days following are a welcome opportunity to reinvent the leftovers. Although there are several dishes involved in the meal, many holiday recipes will make more than is needed to feed your guests. Be sure to store everything tightly covered and in the refrigerator so you can use it all again for the following preparations. Or, if you like, send each of your guests home after the Thanksgiving meal with a few festive, well-labeled, tightly covered, individual containers full of the ingredients and instructions for any of the recipes listed here.

Turkey & Cheddar Panini

Assemble these sandwiches a few hours in advance, then grill them just before serving time.

Butter one side of 8 slices of country-style bread. Spread 1 tablespoon of mayonnaise on the unbuttered side of 4 of the slices. For each sandwich, over the mayonnaise, layer sliced cooked turkey breast with cooked thick-cut bacon and sliced white Cheddar cheese. Top with the remaining bread slice, buttered side up. Preheat a panini grill. Following the grill-manufacturer's directions, cook the panini until the cheese melts and the bread is golden brown, about 2 minutes. Serves 4.

Turkey & Cranberry Sandwiches

Serve this classic treat with Curried Butternut Squash Soup (page 18).

Have ready 8 slices of country-style bread. Spread 1 tablespoon of mayonnaise and 1 teaspoon of Dijon mustard evenly on one side of 4 of the slices. For each sandwich, layer sliced cooked turkey breast with a thin layer of cranberry sauce, a small amount of stuffing, and a small handful of fresh arugula leaves. Top each with 1 slice of bread, cut the sandwiches in half, and serve. Serves 4.

In a frying pan over medium heat, melt 1 tablespoon of butter with 2 tablespoons of olive oil. Add 1 chopped onion and sauté until golden, 4–5 minutes. Add 1½ cups of diced roasted potatoes and 2½ cups of diced cooked turkey and cook, stirring, 1–2 minutes. Top with 1½ cups of stuffing and stir in ⅓ cup of heavy cream. Cook, stirring, until the bottom is crusty, 15–20 minutes. Serves 4.

Turkey & Potato Hash

Serve this breakfast or brunch hash with fried eggs and tomatoes and garnish with fresh flat-leaf parsley.

In a saucepan over medium heat, sauté 1 chopped onion and 2 chopped leeks in 1 tablespoon of canola oil for 7–8 minutes. Add 2 minced garlic cloves, 5 cups of Quick Turkey Stock (page 31), and 1 teaspoon of chopped chipotle chiles in adobo. Bring to a boil over high heat, reduce the heat to medium, and simmer for 8–10 minutes. Add one 15-ounce can of rinsed white beans, ¾ cup of corn, and 2 cups of diced cooked turkey and heat for 2 minutes. Season to taste and serve. Serves 6.

Turkey-Vegetable Soup

The addition of smoky chipotle chiles in adobo adds a Southwestern flair to this hearty, main-dish soup. Round out the meal with a tossed green salad and a loaf of crusty bread.

In a bowl, combine 1 egg yolk with ⅓ cup of sour cream. Add 2 cups of warmed mashed potatoes, ⅓ cup of grated Parmesan cheese, 2 tablespoons of snipped fresh chives, and salt and pepper. Shape the mixture into four 4-inch patties, each ½-inch thick. In a frying pan, melt 1 tablespoon *each* butter and olive oil. Add the patties and sauté, turning once, until browned on both sides, 7–9 minutes, and serve. Serves 4.

Mashed Potato Cakes

Here, leftover mashed potatoes become savory, cheese-laced patties with a crisp, brown crust.

Turkey Know-How

No matter how delicious your appetizers or decadent your pie, the turkey will always take center stage on Thanksgiving Day. Because many cooks roast a whole turkey only once a year, the task can be intimidating to anyone, no matter how experienced. Producing juicy, succulent meat is a challenge when roasting a bird in the oven's dry heat, but the following techniques will help create the ideal bird. Among the secrets to a well-browned turkey with moist meat are brining it (below), using a compound butter or turkey injector (page 30), and checking the temperature with a thermometer (page 106).

BRINING THE TURKEY

Poultry brines contain a specific ratio of salt, sugar, and water, depending on the weight of the bird and the type of flesh, but any combination of garlic, herbs, or spices can be added for flavor. Some brines also include cider, juice, honey, vinegar, beer, or wine.

SELECT A BRINING CONTAINER (top)

Use a nonreactive stockpot made of stainless steel or anodized metal—never uncoated aluminum—that won't react with the acidic ingredients in the brine. Or, use a large, heavy brining bag with a double locking top.

BRINE THE TURKEY (bottom)

As the bird soaks, completely immersed, the salt relaxes the meat proteins, which will then trap the water and flavors inside the flesh for a delicious, moist result.

TRUSSING THE TURKEY

Trussing, or tying, a whole turkey yields a plump roast bird with a tidy shape, making it easier to carve. This technique can also be used for whole roasted chickens and cornish game hens. (However, keep in mind that trussing can cause areas such as the inner thigh joint to receive uneven heat and be underdone when the rest of the bird is ready. Turning the bird in the oven can combat uneven cooking.) When you truss, use sturdy, linen kitchen string, which is less likely than cotton to scorch. Once the bird is done, snip the string off before carving and serving the turkey.

SECURE THE WINGS (top)

Tuck each wing under the shoulder portion of the bird. This can be done when roasting any bird, whether or not you truss it, to keep the wing tips from becoming overly browned.

TIE THE WINGS (middle)

Alternatively, tie the wings securely to the body with a length of kitchen string. Do not tie the string too tightly or else it could mar the skin of the turkey.

TIE THE DRUMSTICKS (bottom)

Cut a 10-inch piece of kitchen string. Stuff the bird, if desired, then cross the drumsticks. Wind the string around each of the drumsticks and then tie the string.

TESTING FOR DONENESS

Checking the internal temperature of the breast and thigh is the best way to know when whole poultry is done, so using an accurate thermometer is crucial. A leave-in thermometer (top) stays in throughout the roasting time and allows you to check the temperature without opening the oven door. An instant-read thermometer (middle and bottom) is inserted near the end of roasting time. These thermometers are interchangeable; choose the one that best suits your needs. A minimum temperature of 160°F will destroy bacteria, but the breast and thigh have different temperatures for ideal doneness.

TEST THE BREAST (top)

To test the breast of a whole bird, insert the thermometer away from the bone, a few inches above the wings. The temperature should be 165°F.

TEST THE THIGH (middle)

To test the thigh of a whole bird, insert the thermometer away from the bone, alongside the cavity under the drumstick. The temperature should be 175°F.

TEST A BONE-IN CUT (bottom)

To test a bone-in cut, such as a whole turkey breast, insert the thermometer into the center of the meatiest part of the cut away from the bone.

CARVING A TURKEY

Once you remove the turkey from the oven, allow it to sit, tented with aluminum foil, for 20–45 minutes before carving. Allowing the bird to rest before you carve it will cause the juices to redistribute evenly throughout the flesh, resulting in a juicy turkey. When carving, the drumstick alone, rather than the entire leg, is removed from each side of the bird, and the wings are initially left in place. The thighs and wings help steady the bird as you carve the breast. Because each drumstick or thigh is larger than a single serving, the meat is sliced from the bone.

REMOVE THE DRUMSTICK (top)

Cut off each drumstick at the knee joint, but do not remove the thigh. If you wish, carve the meat from the drumstick by cutting down to the bone.

CARVE THE BREAST (middle)

Make a deep horizontal cut just above the thigh and wing. Starting at the breastbone, cut downward and parallel to the rib cage for long, thin slices of breast meat.

REMOVE THE THIGH (bottom)

Pry each thigh from the joint, then cut through the joint. Carve off the meat by slicing parallel to the bone. Finally, pry each wing away from the shoulder joints, then cut through the joints.

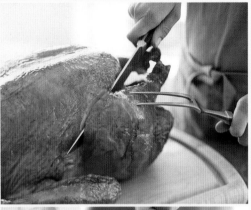

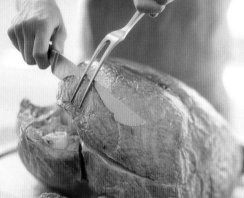

Index

weldonowen

415 Jackson Street, Suite 200, San Francisco, CA 94111
Telephone: 415 291 0100 Fax: 415 291 8841
www.weldonowen.com

Weldon Owen is a division of

BONNIER

WELDON OWEN INC.

CEO & President Terry Newell
VP Sales & Marketing Amy Kaneko
Director of Finance Mark Perrigo

VP and Publisher Hannah Rahill
Executive Editor Jennifer Newens
Associate Editor Juli Vendzules

Associate Creative Director Emma Boys
Art Director Kara Church
Designer Ashley Lima
Junior Designer Anna Grace

Production Director Chris Hemesath
Production Manager Michelle Duggan
Color Manager Teri Bell

Photographer Lara Hata
Food Stylist Kevin Crafts

THANKSGIVING

Conceived and produced by Weldon Owen Inc.
Copyright © 2007 Weldon Owen Inc.

All rights reserved, including the right of reproduction in
whole or in part in any form.

Set in Berkeley Oldstyle, Myriad Pro and Arrus.
Color separations by Embassy Graphics in Canada
Printed and Bound in China by 1010 Printing, Ltd.
First printed in 2007.
10 9 8 7 6 5 4 3

Library of Congress Cataloging-in-Publication data is available.

ISBN-10: 1-61628-164-2
ISBN-13: 978-1-61628-164-9

ACKNOWLEDGMENTS

Weldon Owen wishes to thank the following people for their generous support in producing this book:
Photographer's Assistants Ha Huynh and Heidi K. Ladendorf; **Food Stylist's Assistants** Alexa Hyman and Christine Wolheim;
Copyeditor Sharon Silva; **Proofreader** Melissa Eatough; **Indexer** Ken DellaPenta; and **Editorial Consulting** Julia Humes;
Photographs by Quentin Bacon: Pages 1, 2–3, 6–7, 8–9
Photographs by Tucker and Hossler: Front Cover